Study!

A guide to effective
study, revision and
examination techniques

Study!

A guide to effective study, revision and examination techniques

Robert Barrass

*Principal Lecturer
at Sunderland Polytechnic*

LONDON   NEW YORK
Chapman and Hall

First published 1984 by
Chapman and Hall Ltd
11 New Fetter Lane, London EC4P 4EE
Published in the USA by
Chapman and Hall
733 Third Avenue, New York NY10017

© 1984 Robert Barrass

Printed in Great Britain by Richard Clay
(The Chaucer Press) Ltd, Bungay, Suffolk

ISBN 0 412 25680 0 (Hardback)
ISBN 0 412 25690 8 (Paperback)

British Library Cataloguing in Publication Data

Barrass, Robert
    Study.
    1. Study, Method of
    I. Title
    378'.17'02812   LB2395

    ISBN 0–412–25680–0
    ISBN 0–412–25690–8 Pbk

Library of Congress Cataloging in Publication Data

Barrass, Robert
    Study: a guide to effective study, revision,
and examination techniques

    Bibliography: p. 174
    Includes index.
    1. Study, Method of.   2. College student
orientation.   3. Examinations—Study guides.
I. Title.
LB2395.B33   1984   378'.1702812   84–9558
ISBN 0–412–25680–0
ISBN 0–412–25690–8 (pbk.)

Contents

Preface

Although students of all subjects are judged by their performance in course work and examinations, they may be given little or no advice on study, revision or examination techniques. Most tutors give advice only when they see that it is necessary; and many students feel that they have to do so much studying that they have no time for reading books about it. They prefer to rely on their common sense, to use methods of learning that contributed to their success as pupils at school, and to learn from their own mistakes — if these are recognized. Thus, they pick up advice about study, here and there, as they go along.

Left to themselves many students learn to study effectively, but they may take several months to adjust to the differences between school and college. They continue to gather ideas and to improve their study skills throughout their student life, and so are much better students by the end of their course than they were at the beginning. However, many students still have much to learn about study, revision and examination techniques at the end of their course. It is as if they had come to the end of the game and were still learning the rules. They may then feel, even if they have worked very hard, that they have not achieved their full potential.

Students who know that they are working hard, yet feel that they are not doing as well as they could either in course work or examinations, are likely to benefit most from straightforward advice — because they know that they need help. However, students who are satisfied with their progress can also be helped to do even better work, just as talented athletes can improve their performance when well coached.

It would obviously be best, therefore, in their first few weeks at college, if all students were to consider how to use their study and leisure time. Learning to work effectively (to think, understand, select, organize, and explain or remember) would help them not only at college but also in any career.

The advice in this guide is to help students to think about the way they work and, where necessary, to improve their study, revision and examination techniques. They may read it chapter by chapter (rather than at one sitting) during the first weeks of a course, and then try the techniques recommended. Afterwards they may refer to appropriate chapters, for advice on particular points, throughout their course.

This book may also be used by lecturers and tutors, as an aid to counselling and as a text for a course in study skills. Suggestions for class work are listed in the Index after the entry *exercises and discussion topics*.

DEFINITION OF TERMS

Because the following terms have different meanings in different countries, and even in different colleges in one country, they are defined here.

Assessor or marker: one who assesses the merit of a work and assigns a grade or mark.
Teachers: all people who teach in a school or college.
School or high school: an institution where *pupils*, up to about the age of eighteen, take introductory courses.
College: an institution (college, polytechnic or university) at which *students* take advanced courses.
Term: a period at college between vacations (one third of academic year); compare with *semester* (half academic year).
Class: any organized period of instruction.
Lecturers and *tutors:* people who give lectures and tutorials in a college (although many of them have titles such as professor and doctor).

ACKNOWLEDGEMENTS

I am grateful to my colleague Dr J. B. Mitchell, to Mr Ray Williams of the University of Aston in Birmingham, and to Mr C. de Winter Hebron of Newcastle upon Tyne Polytechnic who read the typescript for this book, for helpful criticisms and suggestions. I also thank my wife for her help, and Mr Adrian Burrows for drawing the cartoons.

Sunderland Polytechnic   Robert Barrass
10 December 1983

1

Study

Different people study effectively in different ways, so no one can tell you how to study, but knowing about ways of working that others have found useful should help you to improve your own study skills. You haven't time to learn only by experience, by making and correcting mistakes.

Obviously, the best time to review your study, revision and examination techniques is at the beginning of your course. You are likely to find that the techniques used at school (where you were taught) are not good enough at college (where it is up to you to learn), and you will want to do as well as possible from the start of your course.

WHY DID YOU DECIDE TO BECOME A STUDENT?

Whatever your reason for coming to college, make the most of this opportunity to participate in college life, to develop your personality, to undertake more demanding studies of subjects in which you are already interested, to develop your ability to think, and to take examinations which will provide a challenge and a measure of your achievement.

Many students who withdraw from a course early, or fail in their examinations, do so because they are not well motivated. Think carefully, therefore, before deciding upon the kind of course to take (see Appendix A) and before deciding which subjects to study in each

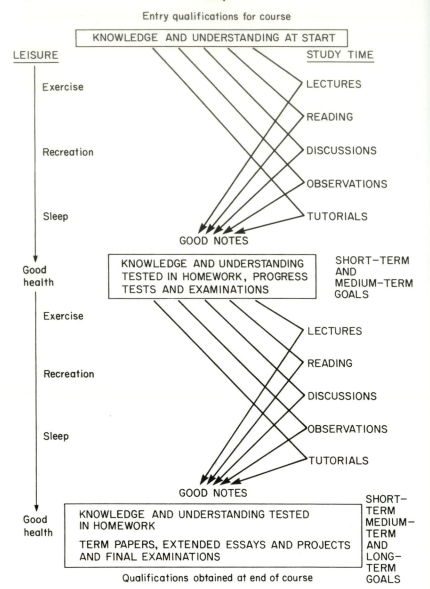

Fig. 1.1 Charting your path through a college course.

year of your course. Then remember that you are taking this course and studying these subjects because you chose to do so.

To maintain your sense of purpose it is best to have clear long- and short-term goals (see Fig. 1.1). For example:

Long term: to progress in a particular career; to achieve grades at the end of your course that are a true reflection of your ability.

Short term: to devote enough time to recreation including your social life; to attend all classes; to complete homework on time; to do your best work.

Immediate: to recognize things that need your attention; to arrange these tasks in order of priority; and then to concentrate on one task at a time.

ARE ALL YOUR SUBJECTS INTERESTING?

You will probably find some subjects interesting from the start, but others may not immediately seem relevant to your main subjects. Consider why these are part of your course. Recognize their importance to you; appreciate their relevance to everyday life or to different careers. Try to relate them to things in which you are already

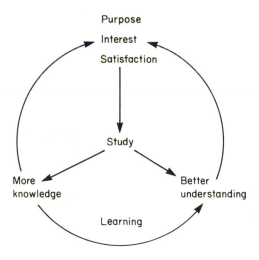

Fig. 1.2 Links between interest, effort, knowledge and understanding.

interested, and remember that they probably do provide a foundation for more advanced work in which you intend to specialize at college or afterwards.

Most people encounter some difficulties when they start a new subject. For example, it may be necessary to learn new words and their meaning. You can develop a positive approach to your studies, in any subject, by being determined to master its special language and other fundamentals. One way or another, making an effort to learn about and understand a subject is your first step towards success in the subject.

You can develop your interest by devoting more time to a subject rather than less. If the lecturer does not capture your interest, look at relevant parts of your textbook which may provide a different approach. If you find your textbook hard-going, look at other

WHAT SHALL I DO NEXT ?

Fig. 1.3 Let your friends know when you will be studying – so that you will not be disturbed at these times.

books: you should be able to find one that is easier to understand and yet suited to your needs. If you still cannot understand anything, ask your tutor for help (see p. 11).

Studying a subject is rather like fitting pieces into a jig-saw puzzle. It is easier to concentrate if you are interested, and as your interest grows you become more and more engrossed. The more you learn, the more you see the subject as a whole and the greater your understanding (see Fig. 1.2). Mastering something that you at first found difficult also boosts your self-confidence in your ability to learn.

Pleasure in study comes from acquiring knowledge, from widening your experience, from developing your ability to solve problems or make judgements, and from your deeper understanding of, for example, works of literature or art, or of people, or of the world. Pleasure also comes from the better results achieved in course work and examinations.

DO YOU STUDY EFFECTIVELY?

Adopting effective study, revision and examination techniques is largely a matter of common sense: if someone suggests possible courses of action it is usually easy to decide which is likely to be the most effective. For example:

1. Do you sit trying to study but feel, after several hours (see Fig. 1.3) that you have not achieved very much? Do you devote most time to the subjects in which most course work is set? Do you spend most time on your favourite subjects? Or do you work to a time-table, studying all subjects but spending most time (as suggested in this chapter) on those that most need your attention?
2. Do you think that being a good student is simply a matter of knowing how to study and how to communicate your knowledge and understanding? Or do you agree that it is just as important to look after yourself (see Chapter 2), and have a good social life (see Chapter 3), if you are to do your best work?

Study may be compared with a game: your purpose is not only to master your subjects but also to score points in course work and examinations. As in playing any game, the first step is to know the rules (see Fig. 1.4).

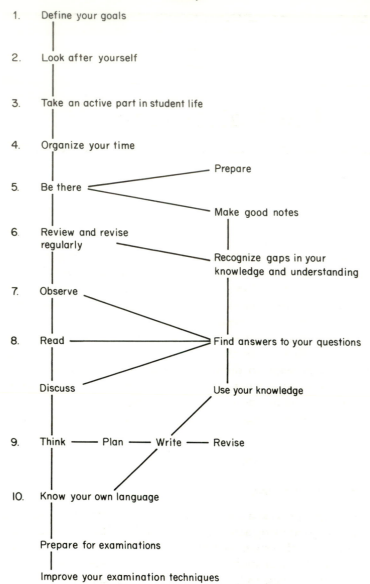

1. Define your goals
2. Look after yourself
3. Take an active part in student life
4. Organize your time
5. Be there
   - Prepare
   - Make good notes
6. Review and revise regularly
   - Recognize gaps in your knowledge and understanding
7. Observe
8. Read — Find answers to your questions
   Discuss
   Use your knowledge
9. Think — Plan — Write — Revise
10. Know your own language

Prepare for examinations

Improve your examination techniques

Fig. 1.4   Basic rules for the study game.

2

Look after yourself

At college you make a fresh start, with different people and in unfamiliar surroundings. The methods of instruction are different and you will need to adopt new techniques that help you to think, to learn and to communicate your knowledge. Most students look forward to making this break from school to college, and enjoy the new experiences that provide both challenges and opportunities.

However, life between the ages of sixteen and twenty-one, when most scholars begin to think of themselves as students, is also a period of transition from adolescent to adult. At this time many students leave home and assume more responsibility for their own actions: there is a change from being cared for to caring for oneself.

LOOKING AFTER YOURSELF

Deciding where to live

Most colleges provide a good working environment. To study most effectively, good living accommodation is also necessary, preferably with a comfortable room in which you can relax by yourself, when you wish to do so, or study without distractions (see p. 34).

It is probably best to live in college accommodation, with other students, at least for your first year at college. This increases your opportunities to make friends with students who are studying different subjects – and so to broaden your interests. In this first year you will also get to know about other kinds of accommodation that may be available, and can consider their advantages and disadvantages.

Wherever you live, you will need a place in which to study effectively – without spending too much time or money on travel. Also, do not allow yourself to be cut off from the opportunities for recreation and friendship which college life provides.

The part-time student, or the student who attends a local college, will probably live at home and have no accommodation problems. However, changes in living arrangements may be needed. It is not possible to work effectively in a room shared with other people who are doing different things (such as talking, listening to the radio or television, or playing games). A student living at home requires the encouragement and support of other members of the family. The same applies if two or three students share a room in college accommodation. The minimum requirement is appropriate conditions (see p. 35) during the hours that must be devoted to private study (see pp. 25–30).

If you cannot go into another room to study when other people are at home, try to fit as much as possible of your study time into your timetable (see p. 24) so that you can study in the reading room of a local library or in the college library. Then study at home at times when you expect other people to be out of the house or busy doing other things in other rooms.

Looking after your money

Mature students who have saved whilst employed, so that they could attend college full-time, or who have to work part-time so that they can attend college full-time, will have experience in handling money and are unlikely to need advice. However, some students may find themselves with a large amount of money of their own for the first time.

It is best to put all this money in an account in which it will earn as much interest as possible, but from which withdrawals can be made either immediately or at short notice. Estimate how much you must spend during the term (e.g. for accommodation, food, clothing and fuel, tuition and examination fees, transport, and books and stationery). Deduct your estimated termly expenditure from your termly income, so that you have an idea of how much you could afford to spend on other things. You can then withdraw a fixed amount each week – if you need it.

Budget to have some money left (plus the interest earned) at the end of term. In this way you can avoid the financial worries that result from being in debt. Remember that even if an overdraft could be obtained from a bank, borrowed money has to be repaid – with interest. Repaying the loan would reduce the amount of money that you would have at the start of the next term. You would then have to borrow more in the second term than in the first, if you were to spend the same amount of money each week as in the first term. Alternatively, to avoid taking out an overdraft in the second term you would have to practise more stringent economies.

Keeping fit for study

You will study most effectively and derive most pleasure from your work and recreation if you are in good health, relaxed, self-confident, and free from worry. On the one hand, anxiety about study (see below) or about personal problems (see p. 19), and mis-use of leisure time, interfere with study and are common causes of failure or under-achievement. On the other hand, success at college depends upon intelligence, hard work, the use of effective study, revision and examination techniques, *and* good health – which depends largely upon having an adequate diet (p. 31), getting enough sleep (p. 31), and developing good personal relationships (see pp. 13–20).

KEEPING UP-TO-DATE WITH YOUR WORK

Anxiety may arise in study because you have difficulty in concentrating, or sit trying to learn your notes but feel after much effort that you cannot remember them, or have difficulty in completing assignments to your own satisfaction in the time available, or feel that you are just not coping with all the different things that must be done. Such anxieties, which result from an ineffective use of time, can usually be overcome, avoided, or relieved, by adopting an active approach to study. Keeping up-to-date depends partly on application (devoting enough time to study and concentrating during hours of study) and partly on organization. If you find yourself in difficulties, consider what you may be doing wrong.

1. Do you need to change your attitude to study (see p. 3)?
2. Do you need to improve your study skills (see p. 5)?
3. Are you devoting too much or too little time to recreation?

It is natural, especially at the start of a new course, to wonder if you will be able to cope with the more advanced work. However, if you have the entry requirements for an advanced course, and if you work hard, study effectively, and have enough recreation, you should succeed in the course and achieve a grade that is a true reflection of your ability. If at first you score low marks in course work, or do not do as well as you expected, do not be discouraged. You have to get used to new methods of working and higher standards. Be positive: try to see where you went wrong (see p. 99 and p. 153) so that you can do better next time.

By working to a timetable (see Tables 4.2–4.4, pp. 27–29) you can ensure that you do devote enough time to study and enough to recreation. Then, by organizing your days (see p. 32), you can plan to use each study period effectively. In this way you will do enough work without over-working.

For any student, anxiety about work that has still to be done may result in too much time being devoted to study – in an attempt to catch up. But overworking, by definition, is counterproductive. Overwork can result in less being achieved, in each hour of study, than would otherwise be possible (see p. 36). Also, overwork can itself be a symptom and then a cause of anxiety. Study will sometimes encroach on your leisure time but do not allow study to become a habit to the extent that you do not take necessary breaks. And do not worry in your leisure time because there are tasks awaiting your attention: this too is counterproductive. In study there are always things to do (see p. 37), and you can avoid anxiety by concentrating on one task at a time and completing the most urgent tasks first.

Do not worry if you feel that you read too slowly and will never be able to read all the things that you are expected to read. Be assured that any student who has passed the qualifying examinations (fulfilling the entrance requirements for an advanced course) is unlikely to be handicapped by slow reading (see p. 83). Then understand that you are unlikely to be expected to read every word of every publication mentioned in lectures or included in reading lists. What is needed is concentration during hours of study (see p. 34) and the use of appropriate reading techniques: scanning, skimming, and a slow critical reading of selected passages. Rapid reading, although useful for some purposes, is not essential. On the contrary, slow reading is part of active study (see p. 84); and slower reading than usual is also to be expected at the start of a course when you may be acquiring additional vocabulary and being introduced to new concepts.

Do not worry if you think that your memory is not as good as that of other students, or that you are not as intelligent. In fact, most people can remember things in which they are interested (see p. 59) and both coursework and examinations are more than a test of memory. Also, it is not easy to assess another person's intelligence. Remember that many students compensate for weaknesses at the start of a course because they are intelligent enough to accept that they must be well organized, work hard, and study effectively.

Satisfaction is derived from overcoming initial difficulties, and persevering through difficult periods, at the end of which you may see connections and things may fall into place. In this respect, studying is like climbing a hill: an all-round view cannot be expected until you reach the top.

Another fact of student life is that the students who enter a course with the best marks in qualifying examinations are not necessarily those who achieve the highest grades at college. Remember this not only if you encounter initial difficulties but also if you do not.

If you feel that the work is not sufficiently demanding or that some subjects seem boring, remember that the set work (assignments or homework) is not all that you should be doing. You must extend yourself: see that you are playing your part in trying to develop an active interest in the work. Otherwise you will find that insufficient application will result in under-achievement.

If, soon after starting a course of study, you find the work un-interesting, or not what you expected, or much too difficult, then perhaps you should be doing something else instead. However, do not give up too easily. Talk to your academic adviser or personal tutor, who will have known other students with similar problems and may reassure you or offer advice. If you wish to change to another course there will be a time limit for doing so. Obviously, it is best if you miss no classes (Fig. 5.1, p. 42) and the beginning of a course is especially important. The later you join a class the harder it will be to fit in and to cope with the work.

Asking for help with study problems

If you encounter a difficulty in your studies, *first try to sort things out for yourself.* For example, think about the problem, look at your lecture notes on the subject and at appropriate parts of textbooks and other sources of information (see pp. 92–97). Ask other students to see if they can explain. Take opportunities to ask questions in class, particularly in tutorials and practical classes.

Most lecturers ask for questions in the last minutes of a lecture, and are pleased to speak to students privately immediately after a class – either to deal with any minor difficulty quickly or to arrange an appointment at a mutually convenient time. Similarly, other members of the academic staff are likely to be available for consultation in their office during normal working hours. With experience you will find when is the best time to call or, if necessary, how to make an appointment. You should feel able to ask your academic adviser or tutor, or any other member of the academic staff whom you find helpful and sympathetic, for help with any study problem, or with any personal problem that could stand in the way of effective study (see p. 19).

3

Friendship

It is best to study alone but to avoid isolation at other times. Having friends with different interests will add interest and variety to your life.

Talking over a difficult point, after a class or after a period of private study, especially with someone who understands it better than you do, will help you with your work. And you will benefit from explaining things to others – just as teachers find that they learn more by teaching than they did, as students, from being taught. You will also find that some students, interested in the same subjects as you are, will have non-academic interests similar to your own.

One advantage of living in college is that you can share accommodation with students who are studying different subjects. They will share your interest in study – and most students will choose to work at the same times (e.g. early in the evening on week days, see Tables 4.2–4.4, pp. 27–29). Then, in coffee breaks and over meals, you have the opportunity to broaden your interests and to talk about other things than work.

Plan to take an active part in student life by participating in some of the activities organized by student clubs and societies. Make a point of doing different things which will help you to meet different people, but do not attempt too much (see p. 23). For example, join a sports club so that you have regular vigorous exercise and join a society that is relevant to your academic interests. Look at notice boards so that you are aware of what is going on in college and in town. Seek relaxation and entertainment that will take your mind away from study. For example, go to a concert or to the theatre. By following your own interests, and by developing new ones, you can broaden your horizons.

If you find study tiring and unsatisfying perhaps this is because you are bored – as a result of devoting too many hours to work or studying ineffectively in other ways, or as a result of not bothering to take an active part in college or town life. Unfortunately, many students do not achieve grades that are a true reflection of their ability, and many fail in examinations, because their studies are adversely affected by anxieties and other causes of ill health. Although these affect study they may be due not to study problems but to personal problems that are the result of a failure to use leisure time effectively.

BEING YOURSELF

Your student days should be a time when your self-confidence and self-reliance increase. As a student, perhaps living away from home for the first time, you have more responsibility than previously for your own actions. You have the opportunity to be yourself and to influence the way your personality develops. However, there is in most people a desire to conform (Fig. 3.1) and soon after arriving at college, if not before, some students begin to dress as if they wished

YOU TOO COULD HAVE A BODY LIKE MINE

Fig. 3.1   At college emulate the successful student, not one with his sights set on failure.

to be recognized as students. They may also be tempted, with more money than previously and with the restrictions of home life removed, to seek new experiences. If they visit student bars, where there are only students and where everyone present seems to be drinking, they may conclude (illogically) that all students drink. In fact many students are not regular drinkers and some avoid alcoholic drinks altogether.

Here is some basic advice about medicines and drugs (including alcohol), which should help you to keep fit for study. The medicines and drugs mentioned are those that you are most likely, as a student, to consider taking.

1. Whereas a medicine containing a carefully measured amount of a drug may cure an illness, all drugs can be harmful.
2. Do not take any medicine or pills unless they have been prescribed for your use, and when you feel ill do not ask for medicine. Let your doctor decide whether or not any treatment is needed.
3. Never exceed the stated dose and do not take two kinds of medicine or pills on the same day – unless your doctor has said that you may do so. Remember also that alcohol is a drug and that you should not have drinks containing alcohol while you are being treated with medicine or pills, unless your doctor has said that it is safe to do so.
4. Never take anyone else's medicine or pills and never allow anyone to take yours.
5. Do not take any medicine or pills if you could be pregnant, unless your doctor knew about this possibility when he prescribed them. Alcohol, cigarettes, and many other drugs, are known to be damaging to an unborn child, and it is important to note that most damage is done in the first few days of a child's development when he or she is very small and the pregnancy has not yet been confirmed.
6. If you think of taking antihistamines for hayfever, remember that they can cause drowsiness, making concentration difficult. They can also make it dangerous to drive a car or handle other machinery.
7. Sleeping pills depress the brain and students who take them are less fit for study, or other work, or for driving a car, on the next day, than they would otherwise be. Try to keep up-to-date with

your studies and get enough relaxation, especially just before going to bed (see p. 31). If you are fresh and free from worry, and have regular sleeping habits, you should not need sleeping pills.

If you seem to take a long time in going to sleep, try to relax so that you can at least benefit from the rest. Let all your muscles relax. Some experts suggest that it is best to think only about relaxing. Alternatively, to take your thoughts away from any current worry, you may prefer to recollect some pleasant experience.

8. Pep pills stimulate the brain and some people take them to overcome a feeling of tiredness, when they should be trying to relax and go to sleep. It is unwise to take pep pills, when you have already studied for long enough, to help you to stay awake and work longer. Extreme physical tiredness and mental depression may be felt when the effects of the pills wear off, so that they have the opposite to the intended effect. There may then be a temptation to take more pep pills to help overcome the feeling of exhaustion resulting from the previous dose. This is a vicious circle. It is best to plan your week (see p. 25) so that you are wide awake all day and ready to sleep at bed-time.

9. Nicotine, the drug in tobacco, is addictive. This is why people who smoke find it difficult to stop – even if they accept that the habit is damaging to their health and that their money would be better spent on other things. However, those who never start smoking do not have the problem of how to stop. Breathing smoke-laden air, which is called passive smoking, is a source of discomfort to non-smokers and it can also damage their health. Fortunately, smoking is usually forbidden in most college buildings, because of the risk of fire and the requirements of insurers. Non-smokers should therefore be able to work in a smoke-free atmosphere.

10. For a student, drinking alcohol regularly is likely to take up much time that would be better spent in other ways, and to be the cause of financial and other worries. Therefore, do not be impressed by the talk of the regular drinker:

'. . . who may have started out with a good intellect but, perhaps because of some fault in his personality, has never studied properly and has never gained the success he expected . . . Naturally he is full of excuses and explanations . . . He is trying to inflate his feeble ego with talk. His examination tips are useless . . . His knowledge of the examiners . . . has never been of any use to him, so why listen and waste your time?'

Passing Examinations, Clifford Allen (1966)

Alcohol affects the brain; and its immediate effects are more marked on those who are not used to the drug than on regular drinkers. It is not a stimulant but a depressant, which adversely affects concentration, removes inhibitions, and increases the risk of accidents. Under the influence of alcohol people are less able to exercise self control and may say and do things that they afterwards regret — perhaps for the rest of their lives. For example, a girl who does not wish to have a baby may be made pregnant by a man whom she would not have chosen as the father of her child; and a man may make pregnant a woman whom he would not have chosen as the mother of his child.

11. Some other forms of drug taking, like drinking alcohol and smoking tobacco, are part of group behaviour. Such drug taking is encouraged by those who are already addicted to the drug, and by those who profit by making and selling the drug.

Anyone who starts taking a drug may soon become addicted to it. As with all bad habits, it is better not to start drug taking than to suffer the physical and emotional harm caused by the drug and to have the problem of trying to break the addiction. It is best, therefore, to refuse any drug that is offered. Apart from other considerations, drugs that come from unreliable sources (because their manufacture and distribution is against the law) are not available in carefully measured doses and their purity is not guaranteed. Their effects are unpredictable and they may well be dangerous. If such drugs are offered by so-called friends you would be well advised to find new friends, who share your values, and to continue being yourself.

PERSONAL RELATIONSHIPS

In all religions people are asked to respect one another, and each person needs moral values that will help to give stability and purpose to life. Parents may exert a good influence, helping their children to tell right from wrong, but in adolescence young people accept full responsibility for their own actions. In learning to live and work with others, they establish their own code of conduct — to exercise self-control, to maintain self-respect, and to show consideration for other people.

Difficulties in personal relationships, which may interfere with study plans and make concentration difficult, are most likely to be the result of romantic attachments. Indeed, the untimely end of a close friendship may cause disappointment and unhappiness, affecting course work adversely and resulting in under-achievement in examinations.

An unplanned pregnancy is likely to be even more disturbing – not only for its immediately adverse effects on study but also for the rest of one's life. For example, it is still very difficult for a woman to bring up a child on her own: most natural fathers do not help. As a student, she may have to give up either her studies or her child.

Many young people do not know as much about sex, or about sexually transmitted diseases, as they appear to think – or as they would like others to think. For example, in Britain, a third of the girls who marry in their teens are already pregnant. However, most sexual relationships in anticipation of marriage do not lead to marriage – and many unwanted pregnancies end not with marriage but with the surgical removal of the developing child. An abortion should not be regarded as an alternative to contraception. After the first twelve weeks of pregnancy it is a major operation; and the later it takes place in pregnancy the more likely is the mother to suffer immediately from depression, bereavement and regrets. If she is a student her studies will be adversely affected both directly, by being interrupted, and indirectly by the emotional upsets.

Young people who do not want to have children should either avoid sexual intercourse or use an effective method of contraception. They should also be aware of the world-wide upsurge of venereal diseases – especially among young people. These sexually transmitted diseases are caught by those who give opportunities for sexual intercourse, outside marriage, and by those who take these opportunities. Those who are willing to have sexual encounters (heterosexual or homosexual) with people they do not know very well, have probably had similar casual encounters with other people. Even if clean and apparently healthy, they may have one of these diseases.

It takes some time for symptoms to develop, and during this time an infected person may pass on the disease. Anyone who suspects that they could have caught a venereal disease should go to see a doctor at once, without waiting for symptoms to develop. Otherwise permanent damage may result before the treatment starts. Without treatment, gonorrhoea causes pain and may make a man or woman sterile. And without treatment, syphilis may be followed, years later, by heart disease, blindness, madness and paralysis. At all stages of the infection, venereal diseases may be passed on to others and a pregnant woman may infect her child.

COPING WITH PERSONAL PROBLEMS

It is easier to avoid difficult situations, or to cope with them, if you have clear long-term objectives and have considered how different courses of action (for example, in relation to drugs and sex) could affect your chances of attaining them. Having decided what you want to do with your life, both as a student and after leaving college, you are prepared if anyone tries to persuade you to do anything against your will.

You are entitled to your own opinions as to what is right and wrong, and should be prepared to stand up for yourself. It is best to stick to your principles and not lower your self-imposed standards to conform with what appears to be the behaviour of the majority, or with what you think are the opinions of the majority. You can maintain your self-respect, and the respect of most other people, if you have the strength of character to do what you consider to be right in any situation.

Although, if you have problems, they are likely to be similar to those encountered by other students, you will need to consult other sources for more specific and more detailed information than can be given in a book such as this. Also, if you have difficulty in finding the answer to a question, or the solution to any problem, do not be afraid to ask for help. Especially when you are new at college, you may need advice and the people you would previously have consulted may not be readily available. You may not know where to turn for help. This is why you have an academic adviser or personal tutor who, if unable to help directly, may suggest that you should see another member of the academic staff, or help you to make an appointment to see a member of the student advisory services (such as a students' counsellor or careers officer, or a member of the student health services).

If you have any personal problem, by all means try to think of a satisfactory solution. It is usually a good idea to sleep on a problem: things may seem different in the morning. But do not brood on things for too long. Writing a letter home or talking over any problem with a sympathetic listener – a parent, a tutor, a friend – may help in itself. The sooner you either find a solution or decide that you just have to accept things as they are, the sooner your worries may be removed or relieved, leaving you free to concentrate on your studies.

4

Make good use of your time

At school, time is allocated to organized classes, including recreation periods, and perhaps also to private study. Teachers set definite tasks for homework. Pupils may be able to learn all they need to know about a subject from one teacher and one textbook; and they may be told exactly what they must know for an examination.

At college some of your time is still organized for you. You are expected to attend lectures, tutorials, seminars, practical classes, field trips, and other educational visits; and some tasks are set for homework. There are no time-tabled periods for games, athletics or physical training, but the facilities are there if you wish to use them. Also, there are many clubs and societies that you could join. Therefore, unless you are well organized you could easily devote too little or too much time to study, or too much to procrastination.

ACCEPT THAT LEARNING IS YOUR RESPONSIBILITY

The last years at school are a period of transition. Senior pupils should need less help than previously and should be accepting more responsibility for their own progress – as they learn to be students. The poor performance of some students at college is the result of their failure to take the initiative (see Fig. 1.4, p. 6).

At school it is the teacher's job to capture and hold the pupil's interest. A teacher asks questions to make everyone think, to check that they understand, and to revise previous work. But at college a lecturer's task is to stimulate your thinking and help you to know what to study. It is up to you to ask questions when necessary. Learning is your responsibility. You are unlikely to be told exactly what is expected of a good student, but you can benefit from the comments of different lecturers and from reading the works of different authors. Be prepared to consider ideas and advice from many sources and to assess your own progress.

After school, on a more advanced course, the work should be more demanding. A higher standard is expected and a different approach. Study is interesting and rewarding – but it *is* work. Your success as a student, as in your career, will depend upon your interest and enthusiasm (motivation); your ability to think, understand, select, organize, remember, and explain; and upon how hard you work, how effectively you work, and how effectively you use your leisure time. It is not possible to place these things in order of importance (see Fig. 4.1). However, note that although by hard work you can compensate for deficiencies in other respects, you can make your work much easier by good organization – so that you make effective use of your study and leisure time.

At the start of your first year at college, after looking at course outlines, syllabuses, past examination papers, and timetables, prepare a plan showing terms and vacations for all years of your course. Include the times and titles for courses of lectures, for courses of practical work, for field studies, for project work, and for tests and examinations. Referring to this plan will help you to see at a glance how your work at any time fits in to the course as a whole. Having a plan should help you to organize your work as a whole and to organize, for example, your first year's work towards progress tests and examinations (see Table 4.1).

However, study is not the only activity in a student's life: you also contribute to and benefit from college life. In college clubs and societies, in addition to being with friends who have similar interests to your own, you may be able to gain valuable experience of committee work, of speaking in public, and (if you wish) of the duties of a club secretary or chairman. In both academic and non-academic activities you gain experience of getting along well with people and developing good working relationships and friendships based upon mutual respect and understanding.

You may have other commitments, especially if you live at home, and there will be attractions in the town. You will not, therefore,

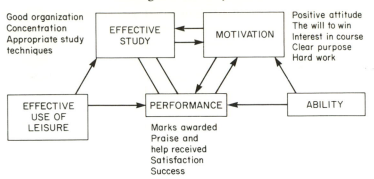

Fig. 4.1 Some factors that influence performance. The marks and grades awarded are not just an indication of ability. Students also differ in their starting point (influenced by their home background and previous education), in their motivation, and in their use of time.

have time to do all those things that you might like to do. It is important to consider this at the start of your course so that you can *have a social life that does not take up too much of your time.*

Non-academic interests contribute to personal development: without them you are likely to become narrow-minded and dull. Furthermore, when you come to look for employment, both your academic achievements and your non-academic interests will indicate to an employer the kind of person you are.

To do well at college most students have to exercise self-discipline, and the qualification obtained may indicate both ability and perseverance. Your success at one kind of work (being a student) may be taken as an indication of your ability to tackle another (as an employee). This is especially important if you change your mind about what you would like to do after leaving college, or if you are unable to obtain employment in your chosen career. Most employers are looking for employees with a variety of interests who have more to offer than a paper qualification.

By planning your course, year by year and week by week, you can keep a sensible balance between academic and non-academic interests. You can plan not just your studies but the whole of your student life. On the one hand you will not want to feel a slave to a rigid timetable; but, on the other hand, if you fall behind with your studies you will have to work even harder than usual to catch up. It is best to *organize your timetable to suit yourself*, so that you can work more

Table 4.1 First year studies at college and in vacations

Term 1		
(11 weeks)	Organized classes	Keeping up-to-date with set work and completing other necessary studies
	3 weeks vacation	Revision of first term's work
Term 2		
	Mid-sessional test	Keeping up-to-date with set work and
	Organized classes	completing other necessary studies
	4 weeks vacation	Revision of first year's work
Term 3		
	Organized classes completed	Final revision for first year examinations
	First year examinations	
	12 weeks vacation	Holiday (2 weeks)
		Private study and recreation
		Consolidation and background reading
		Preparation for second year's work
		Holiday (1 week)

effectively and have more leisure time than would otherwise be possible. If you think that you have so much to do that you have no time to spend on planning, be assured that your timetable will enable you to use your time more effectively and so save time later.

Many students who do not organize their time effectively, and do not communicate very well in writing, nevertheless manage to pass their examinations. In this sense they are successful, but it is not possible to know how much more successful they might have been had they used better study, revision and examination techniques. Nor can we know how many of those who fail might have passed if they had worked more effectively and been better able to display their knowledge in examinations. We know only the grade obtained, not what might have been.

ORGANIZE YOUR YEAR

Your purpose, as a student, should be to master all your subjects. To do this it is necessary to work steadily throughout the year, not just in the last few weeks before your examinations. Keep up-to-date with course work, week by week, so that you have time to think about each subject, to undertake background reading, and to learn as you go along.

If your days and weeks are well organized, you should be up-to-date with your studies at the end of each week and, therefore, at the end of each term. You can then use each vacation, depending upon its length, as an opportunity for a short break from your studies – for a few days in a short vacation or for two or three weeks in a long vacation. But remember that college vacations are not intended to be holidays. Nor should they be devoted entirely to paid employment.

Most full-time students spend a little more than half of each year at college. In vacations, therefore, allocate many hours to active study to keep each subject alive in your mind and to build upon the foundations laid at college. Do not waste time. Without planning at the start of each vacation, and exercising self-discipline every day, you may find that the time slips away and you achieve little or nothing. You can easily lose an hour by getting up late, then lose another reading a newspaper or magazine after breakfast, and so on. Instead, be positive: regard each vacation as *an opportunity for revision, consolidation, and background reading,* as well as for recreation, so that you come to feel that you know your subjects and are well prepared for the next term's work (see Table 4.1).

ORGANIZE YOUR WEEK

At the start of each term, prepare a timetable or schedule that includes all your organized classes and the times that you intend to devote to private study. These things should come first in your order of priorities. Then include any other commitments and take care to leave enough time for recreation (see Tables 4.2–4.4) and for sleep. Note that there are 168 hours in each week and consider how you will use them. You *should* spend 56 hours asleep, and you *could* devote 56 hours to study – which would leave 56 hours for recreation and other essential activities.

A full-time student who is at college for eight hours each day, and allows one hour for lunch, can work for 35 hours each week – and would need to study for another 14 hours each week (in the evenings and at week-ends) to make a 49 hour working week. This means, in term time, that a student of science or engineering, with 24 hours of organized classes, could devote 25 hours to private study; and an arts student, with 12 hours of organized classes could devote 37 hours to private study.

A part-time student who is engaged in other work for seven hours on each week day, and who has three hours of organized classes on each of two evenings, will need to allocate eight hours to private study to make a 49 hour working week. Part-time study is not easy (see p. 172), but some of the subjects studied may be directly relevant to the student's paid employment and others may provide a complete change from other work, and so may offer, in themselves, absorbing interests and opportunities for recreation and relaxation. The part-time student may decide, therefore, to allocate more than eight hours each week to private study.

Tables 4.2–4.4 are the timetables of three full-time students. The Diploma student has classes for twenty hours each week and devotes twenty hours to private study: a well motivated student would probably do more. The arts degree student has only twelve hours of organized classes and clearly could achieve a better balance between work and recreation and yet devote more time to private study. This student is spending too much time on study on some days but not enough on others. The engineering degree student might be well advised to take a break earlier in the week (perhaps on Wednesday evening) and to study for at least three hours at the weekend in this final year. Consider *your own* timetable in this way: are you making effective use of your time?

Your timetable is your schedule for work. Instead of writing the words library or study (as in Tables 4.2–4.4) decide which subjects you will study in each private study session – so that you can allocate enough time to each of your subjects. Make your plan and modify it in the light of experience; then do your best to stick to it, so that it is more than a statement of your good intentions. As far as possible, devote the same times each week to the same subjects so that you can prepare for classes, check your notes after classes, write laboratory reports promptly etc. *You will not* then make the mistake of devoting too much time to your favourite subjects at the expense of weaker subjects, on which you should probably be spending more of your time.

Plan ahead as far as you can so that you keep up-to-date in all subjects and hand in set work on time (see Table 4.5, p. 33). However, do not make the common mistake of thinking that your set work is all that you need to do. Being a student means that *you make*

Table 4.2 Timetable of a student in the first year of a two year Diploma course in Business Studies

	M	T	W	T	F	S	S
1	S BO	S BE	L Mk	L BO	L DP	Study	
2	S BO	S BE	L Mk	L CL	L DP	Study	
3	Library	L BE	S Mk	S BT	Library		
4	Library	Library	S CL	S BT	Library		
1	L BT	Library		L CL	Library		
2		GA		Library	Library		
3	S DP	GA		Library	Library		
4				Library			
1	Study		Study	Study			Study
2	Study		Study	Study			Study
3							

Key

L = Lecture
S = Seminar
XXXX = Break

BO = Business organization
BE = Business environment
BT = Business techniques
GA = Group assignment

CL = Consumer law
DP = Data processing
Mk = Marketing

the decisions about what needs to be done: you should be doing more than is demanded.

Do not waste time. Behave as if you were employed in one of the professions and stick to *self-imposed* hours of work. On weekdays, if you have no organized class, *make an early start in the library* and

Table 4.3 Timetable of student in the second year of a Combined Arts Degree course with Geography and Literature as main subjects

	M	T	W	T	F	S	S
1	Study		Library	Library	L AL		
2			Library	Library	L VL		
3	S AL	L VB	Library	Library	S VL		
4		S VB					
1	Library	L WE					
2	Library	S WE	Library				
3	Library	L DS	Library	L WR			Study
4		S DS	Library	L WR			Study
1	Study	Study	Study	Study			
2	Study	Study	Study	Study			
3	Study	Study	Study	Study			

Key

L = Lecture	AL = American Literature	DS =	Development and Society
S = Seminar	VL = Victorian Literature	WE = Western Europe	
XXXXX = Break	VB = Legacy of Victorian Britain	WR = Water Resources	

plan to make good use of free periods during the day. These are not times when you should be doing nothing: they are opportunities for study or for recreation. Do not spend more than ten to fifteen minutes, regularly, on tea or coffee breaks. Otherwise you will find that hours slip away.

Table 4.4 Timetable of student in the final year of a Degree course in Electrical and Electronic Engineering

	M	T	W	T	F	S	S
1	Project	L Net	L MSD	Study	Lab		
2	Project	L Com	S MSD		Lab		
3	Project	Library	Library	L Net	Lab		
4	Project	Library	Library	Library	Library		
1	Project	L Man	L Com	L Con	S		
2	Project	S Man	L Elec	S Con	S		
3	Project		S Elec	Study	Project		
4	Study	Study	Study				
1	Study	Study	Study	Study	Study		
2	Study	Study	Study	Study	Study		
3							

Key L = Lecture   Net = Network   Elec = Electronic engineering
     S = Seminar   Com = Communication
     Lab = Practical class   Man = Management   Con = Control
     XXXX = Break   MSD = Microprocessor System Design

If you expect to have an hour free during the day, there is time to find a quiet spot, complete forty minutes of effective study, and then walk to your next class. You may think that not much can be achieved in forty minutes but this is more time than you would be allowed in an examination for thinking about a question, planning and writing your answer, and checking your work. There are many kinds of tasks that can be completed in less than an hour (see p. 32), providing only that you avoid distractions and know exactly what you want to achieve in the time. Some of your study sessions, during the day, will be longer than forty minutes; in these you can do more.

On week days, when you study in the evening, it is probably better to devote three hours to study and one to recreation than to try to work for four hours. You could not achieve twice as much in four hours as you could in two; and you will probably achieve little more in four hours than you could in three. At weekends it is probably best to study in one, two or three-hour sessions, to ensure that you have longer periods for recreation, and to give some thought to your next week's work.

Try to arrange regular times that you will spend with friends, in different activities, so that they know when you are studying – and that you will not want to be disturbed at these times.

Exercise and health

If you live near enough, take exercise every day by walking or cycling to college. Try to allocate time, every week, to longer walks or to more active exercise such as running, swimming or a sport. Your body is used more fully during exercise than when you are resting. In swimming, for example, your leg and arm muscles are used repeatedly, you breathe faster and deeper, and your heart beats faster than when you are inactive. Exercise contributes to a state of readiness to act in all your muscles, and after exercise you are more alert. You have a feeling of well-being and are refreshed (Fig. 4.2).

Exercise is important throughout life, because it contributes to physical fitness and to mental alertness, but it is especially important while you are a student. Without exercise, preferably in the open air, you may become lethargic, spending too much time sitting – in lectures, in a library, and during hours of private study. You are most likely to become lethargic in the weeks before an examination when revision is important and you may feel that you have no time for recreation. But this is one time when you need exercise every day to help you remain mentally alert.

Food and health

Eating regular meals, including a variety of foods, contributes to

WHAT IS THIS LIFE FULL OF CARE?

Fig. 4.2 Recreation, like work, is most satisfying if it provides a change and a challenge, and is enjoyable.

good health. Breakfast, after about eight hours without food, is a most important meal which should give you a good start to the day. But take care not to eat too much at lunch or you will be sleepy in lectures when you want to be alert; and over-eating in the evening may make concentration difficult during hours of study and then make sleep more difficult at night.

Sleep and health

Anyone over the age of eighteen needs about eight hours sleep at night. Working late into the night may be necessary from time to time, and talking into the early hours may be an occasional pleasure, but even one late night will affect your work on the next day. As a student, therefore, it is a good idea to get into the habit of going to bed by eleven so that you are ready to get up at seven. This is especially important in the weeks preceding an examination when you must be well organized – with regular times for study, recreation and sleep.

At the end of an evening's study, try to relax before going to bed. A short walk in the fresh air can be very refreshing. Conversation or light reading, which help you to think about other subjects, will provide a change after study. A hot drink will help you to relax.

ORGANIZE YOUR DAY

Allocate some time to going over class work, while it is fresh in your mind, to make sure that your notes are clear and correct. Check that you will be able to understand them later but do not get into the time-wasting habit of copying out notes just to make them neater. Devote some time to regular revision (see p. 61) and to thinking about each subject, with your lecture notes as a guide to what is required. Spend enough time on learning and on background reading. If you have been given an outline of the course, in which the topics to be considered each week are listed, spend some time at the week-ends on preliminary reading. Allocate some of your time to preparing for practical classes, seminars and tutorials, so that you are better able to understand your work and to contribute to discussions.

Before you finish work each day, clear your working surface. Consider what you have achieved and look at your timetable or work-plan for the next day.

1. Make a list of any engagements or other things that you must do.
2. List a limited number of study tasks that you expect to complete.
3. Decide how you will use any free periods during the day.
4. Put together any books, papers or other materials that you will need.

You must have a particular piece of work in mind for each study session, so that you know not only what you will do but also when and where. You can then complete the most urgent tasks first, avoid distractions (such as conversation or the temptation to tackle some less urgent but more intriguing problem), and concentrate on one thing at a time. You will not then waste time, when you sit down to work, wondering what to do next (see Fig. 1.3, p. 4).

Listing tasks is a matter of accepting that you cannot do all the things that you might like to be doing, recognizing what needs to be done, and establishing an order of priority. Here is the difference between a pupil who has to be told what to do and a student who can see what needs to be done. For example, a student will still be given clearly defined pieces of homework but within each of these it is possible to recognize smaller tasks.

1. Think, and prepare notes of ideas and information that must be included in your answer (see p. 65).

2. Prepare a topic outline for your answer (see p. 66).
3. Fill gaps in your knowledge (see p. 51) and, if necessary . . .
4. Undertake background reading to get additional ideas.
5. Revise your topic outline, and . . .
6. Write your answer (see p. 105).
7. Check and, if necessary, revise your work (see p. 111).

Allocate time to each of these tasks (see Table 4.5) and try to ensure that each task is one that can be completed in this time.

Table 4.5 Answering a question in course work

Tasks		Activities	Minutes	Count down
	Work set on Monday			
1		Thinking		
	Monday evening			
2		Planning	30	7
3	Tuesday morning	Searching	40	6
4	Wednesday evening	Reading	30	5
	Thursday			4
5		Revising plan	10	
	Friday morning			3
6		Writing	30	
	Saturday			2
7	Sunday morning	Checking	10	1
	Monday			0
		Total*	150	

*Note   In course work two and a half hours could be well spent on a composition that in an examination would have to be completed in a much shorter time

Recognizing what needs to be done enables you to organize your studies and to do the best work of which you are capable in the time available.

This positive approach to your studies means, even in dealing with set work, that you are in control. You make the decisions, and have no need to worry about the possibility that you may not complete the work satisfactorily and on time. Instead of struggling to cope as you go along, it pays to plan ahead. Such anticipation will increase your self-confidence and help you to provide a basis for effective learning.

As you work on your notes you may recognize gaps in your knowledge and understanding, and these can be noted as things that need your further attention.

> Look up the name of . . . or the title of the book by . . .
> Find out more about . . .
> Read chapter . . . of textbook on . . . before lecture on . . .

Keep to your timetable each day but be prepared to renumber tasks in your list of things to do, to revise your order of priority when necessary, so that you can concentrate on the most important or most urgent tasks *one at a time*. If you do not complete any task in the time that you had allocated to it, look at your list when you prepare for your next day's work. Uncompleted tasks can then be carried forward and not forgotten. Working to a timetable, and with a list of things to do, does not mean being inflexible. At times some subjects will require more attention than others, and some tasks will take longer than you expected.

Your numbered list of *things to do* helps you to organize your day. Crossing off each task as it is completed is a source of satisfaction and an indication that you are making progress; and adding a task to the list, so that you will not forget it, leaves you free to concentrate on a higher task in your order of priority.

CONCENTRATE DURING HOURS OF STUDY

If you have difficulty in concentrating during hours of study, here are some basic rules that will help you to improve your study habits. See also Fig. 4.3).

1. Having prepared a timetable, *start each study session on time*.
2. *Try to study* in a quiet part of a library, in an empty classroom, or in your own room, *where you expect to be free from distractions* and interruptions.
3. *Make good use of study facilities in a library*: the atmosphere should be conducive to study. Also, it is a good idea to study regularly where other people are working because this should help you to concentrate and give you practice in working under something like examination conditions.
4. *Maintain a good posture* so that you can sit comfortably during

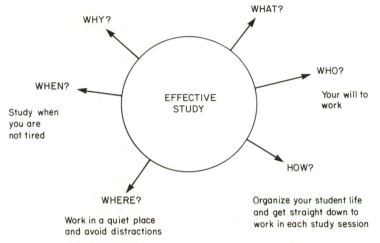

Work with a long-term purpose and recognize what needs to be done at each stage in your course and in each study session

Study subjects in which you are interested and develop an active interest in all aspects of your work

WHY?

WHAT?

WHO?

WHEN?

Your will to work

EFFECTIVE STUDY

Study when you are not tired

HOW?

WHERE?

Work in a quiet place and avoid distractions

Organize your student life and get straight down to work in each study session

Fig. 4.3 Factors that contribute to motivation – your will to work – which is the basis for effective study.

long periods of active study. Sit upright and try to ensure that your chair and working surface are the right height for you (see Fig. 9.1, p. 100).

5. *Make sure that you have enough space* for your notes and other necessary books or papers (see Fig. 4.4). Some people get used to working amidst a familiar jumble, but you are advised not to allow your working surface to become cluttered with things that are not required for the task in hand, and which can provide only distractions.

6. *Make sure that your working surface is sufficiently and evenly illuminated*; and that the light is not in your eyes. Daylight is best and, if you are right-handed, the light should come from your left (as in Fig. 4.4). Adjust the light to suit your purpose: you will need more for preparing an accurate diagram than for writing or reading. Do not work in intense light and avoid glare from the working surface or from papers. For reading, support the book at an angle so that all words are about equidistant from your eyes.

If you normally read quickly but find that you are reading

GET STRAIGHT DOWN TO WORK!

Fig. 4.4 Avoid distractions: sit in a quiet place and keep to hand just the things you need for a particular task.

slowly, this may be due to fatigue. Reading critically and making notes will help you to maintain your concentration, but do not read for too long without a break. A defect of vision (or hearing) may be a great handicap for a student and it is advisable to see a doctor at once if you suspect that you may need help.

7. Before starting to study, try to *ensure that the room is well ventilated and at a suitable temperature.* You are unlikely to be able to maintain attention for long in a badly ventilated and over-heated room.

8. *Undertake problem solving, planning and other demanding tasks* and work at your weaker subjects (which you find most difficult) *when you are at your best.* This will probably be in the morning or at the start of an evening's work. Tasks that you are looking forward to, or which you expect to be straightforward, can be done in the second and third hours of an evening's study session. It is better to get up an hour earlier to study, in the morning, than to stay up an hour later at night. In the evening it is best to start work early, to finish early, and to do something

different during the last hour before going to bed.

9. *Make each task an activity*, and use different strategies for learning (i) so that you are always aware of your course and of each subject as a whole as well as in parts, and (ii) so that an evening's study comprises different kinds of activity.

Long term: obtaining an overview

<u>Survey</u> syllabus for your course on . . . to see how the part you are currently studying fits into the whole.

<u>Look</u> at contents pages of books on . . . to see different approaches to the subject and its scope.

<u>Look</u> at titles of lectures included in a particular course, to put each lecture in perspective.

<u>Review</u> your progress and revise regularly.

Short term: moving forward step by step

Gathering and processing information

<u>Prepare</u> for classes on . . .

<u>Check</u> notes after classes on . . .

<u>Look up</u> references mentioned in class on . . .

<u>Find</u> more information about . . .

Concentrated study

<u>Read</u> critically chapter . . . of . . .

<u>Incorporate</u> relevant points in lecture notes on . . .

<u>Plan</u> answer to question on . . .

<u>Solve</u> problems on page . . . of . . .

<u>Write</u> . . .

<u>Summarize</u> . . .

With such clearly defined tasks you know exactly what has to be done and you know when each task is complete. You will be able to sit down and get straight on with the task you have planned for this study session. Keep your mind on your work: avoid daydreaming. If you regard each task as a challenge, completing it will be a source of satisfaction. But this will be true only if each task is one that you can complete in the time you have allocated to it.

10. On completing each task, *review your work* and check for accuracy, orderliness and completeness. Consider what you have achieved and make a note of what must be done next time you study this subject. Devote a few minutes to revision. Put away the books and papers relating to this task before you start work on the next.

11. *Do not mistake boredom for fatigue*. You will find it easy to concentrate on a subject that interests you. Developing an active interest in all subjects of your course (see p. 68) is therefore the basis for effective study. See Fig. 4.3, p. 35).

12. *Do not work for too long at one task*. Most people concentrate best for the first twenty minutes or so. Therefore, so that you can maintain attention and avoid daydreaming, try to break your work into tasks that can be completed in under an hour (see Table 4.5). Setting a time limit also provides an incentive for you to start on time and to work steadily at each task.

13. Organize your studies so that successive tasks are *different kinds of activity*: solve, plan, check, make notes on, review, write, read etc.

14. From time to time, *take a break of two or three minutes*. If you just stand, take a few deep breaths, exercise your arms, and walk around the room a few times, this should help you to maintain attention when you resume work.

    Towards the end of the second hour of a three hour study session, take a 10-minute break. Move away from your work and do something different. Take such longer breaks at the end of one piece of work (as you would at the end of a lecture), so that you have the satisfaction of completing one task and can make a fresh start on the next.

    The first hour of a two hour study session may be spent as follows: 40 minutes for *study*, 10 minutes to *review* and *revise*, 5 minutes to put away your papers and prepare for the next task, and 5 minutes for a break. The second hour may comprise 40 minutes for *study*, 10 minutes to *review* and *revise* and put away your papers, and 10 minutes for a break. Then do not allow this break to last more than 10 minutes: start your third hour's study on time. You may find that some of your best ideas come to mind during short breaks in your studies, in moments of quiet relaxation and contemplation, and during recreational activities when your attention is on other things (see p. 106).

15. You may have difficulty in concentrating on your studies because of some anxiety – which may or may not be connected with your studies (see p. 9 and p. 19). *Try to deal with this problem as soon as you can* so that you will be able to concentrate better on your work. Similarly, if something is demanding your attention (perhaps you have to make a telephone call or

write a letter) then it is best to do this at once and quickly *before* the time you have allocated for study, so that it can be crossed off your list of things to do.

Exercising self-discipline and being well organized, with a positive approach to the course as a whole, in maintaining good study habits week by week, in allocating study periods to definite tasks, and in adopting effective study and revision techniques, will help you to concentrate on your work and to achieve more than would otherwise be possible. You will also be able to relax in your leisure time. In consequence, you should find study more satisfying and recreation more enjoyable.

Some good students may seem to learn without effort and to work without a written timetable, but this is not to say that their work is unorganized. The organization may be in their minds. They recognize, perhaps without writing a list, what needs to be done and which tasks must be done first. They have time for leisure activities but do not waste time. However, to be so well organized (or perhaps to be better organized) most students need the self-imposed discipline of keeping to a fairly rigid written timetable and the reminder provided by a numbered list of tasks arranged in order of priority.

5

Make good lecture notes

In lectures you spend most of your time listening and making carefully selected notes, but in other group activities (especially in tutorials and practical classes) you receive more personal attention. In private study, although working alone, you use your lecture notes as well as books and other records prepared by other people. The distinction between group activities and private study is not therefore clear cut. One supports the other, and both provide opportunities for learning.

In spite of the central place of your lecture notes in active study, in drawing all aspects of your work together and as an aid to learning (see Fig. 8.2, p. 89), and in spite of the time devoted to making notes in class (see p. 44) and to improving them afterwards (see p. 52), you are unlikely to be given advice on how to make notes. Furthermore, in contrast with other aspects of course work, you will not have the opportunity to benefit from other people drawing attention to mistakes. This is because your lecture notes are normally regarded as being for your eyes only. It is worth taking a critical look at your own notes, therefore, but first consider:

1. The importance of attending all organized classes.
2. The value of lectures in study.
3. How other students make notes during lectures, tutorials and seminars.

BEING THERE

You would be wise to look at the syllabus for your course, upon which examinations should be based, but your best and only complete guide to the course content (especially when examinations are set and marked internally) is provided in the organized classes which you are expected to attend. Your intention, therefore, should be to attend all organized classes, to arrive on time, and to listen carefully to every word. There is no substitute for being there. Good students attend regularly — and those who miss classes are usually losing interest in the course, or are over-confident, and are unlikely to achieve grades that are a true reflection of their ability.

The notes you make during organized classes are your own summary of what was said. They are of use to you not only for what is recorded but also as an aid to your memory. Looking at these notes, later, you will be able to remember much more of what was said by the lecturer. You should also have a record of the questions asked by yourself, and by other students, and of the lecturer's replies.

You cannot make up for missing a lecture by reading a book or by copying notes made by another student. Obviously, another student's notes cannot remind you of things that happened in the class that you did not attend. Also, students differ in their knowledge at the start of a class, in what they select for inclusion, and in the way they make notes. Another student's notes may also be an incomplete record of even the lecturer's main points and they may contain mistakes and misunderstandings. If they contain the student's own comments you may be unable to distinguish the lecturer's words from the student's thoughts. If necessary therefore, after an unavoidable absence, look at another student's notes and make what you can of them. Obtain exact details of any set work. Then, after apologizing for your absence, ask the lecturer how you should attempt to fill the gap in your own notes (see Fig. 5.1).

THE VALUE OF LECTURES IN STUDY

Reading a book on a subject is not an alternative to attending a course of lectures on the same subject. The lecture and the textbook are complementary: they should be used in different ways.

At the start of a course of lectures you will find it helpful to copy the appropriate part of the syllabus on to the first page of your

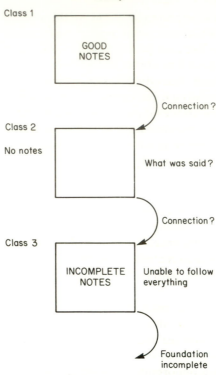

Fig. 5.1 Some consequences of missing one class. You benefit less than you should from the first class; you miss the second; and you may not fully understand the third. Your foundation for further study is incomplete.

lecture notes for the course, so that you will be aware of the scope of the studies proposed. But note that the lecturer may spend more time on some aspects than on others; and may leave you to deal with some things entirely on your own.

In the first lecture of a course a good lecturer will answer your questions: why (purpose of course), what (content of course), and when (development of subject week by week). This is rather like giving you a map and a timetable for a journey, so that you will know your route, how you are progressing, and when you should arrive at your destination. The first lecture is therefore important, but so are the others – each of which will probably be devoted to one aspect of the subject. And the last lecture, in which no new ground may be covered, is one that no student can afford to miss (see p. 149).

You will find it helpful to have a list of the topics to be considered in each week of the course, with suggestions for preliminary reading. However, some lecturers prefer to say, at the end of each lecture, what the next one will be about. In a well planned course the lecturer acts as a pace setter. Attending classes, therefore, should help you to move smoothly through the course and to complete the necessary studies in time for your examinations. Being there helps you to know what the lecturer considers to be the most important points for you in this course. Listening to the lecture, and participating in any discussion, helps you to think about your subject and to move forward in an organized way – faster than would be possible if you worked alone.

Listening to a lecture, *looking* at words written on a blackboard or at other visual aids, *taking a critical interest*, and *recording* carefully *selected* and well *organized* notes, are all *aids to active study*. These activities help you to maintain attention, to pick out key ideas, to recognize an orderly pattern in what is being said, to learn, and to remember.

Creative thinking is aided by concentrating on main points, concepts and ideas, rather than detail. *Learning is aided* by the use of different senses: you see and hear, and you feel the pen moving in your hand as you repeat (by writing or drawing) those things that you consider most important. *This repetition helps you to remember.* For all these reasons, attending lectures regularly and making good notes is probably the most effective study technique for introducing new material and developing your interest. You absorb the most ideas and information for the least work, and you are well placed to continue your studies.

Do not lose interest in a lecture if you think that you have heard it all before. If you have done some preliminary reading you will expect to be on familiar ground. This should help you to appreciate the lecturer's approach; to select and note, particularly, anything that is not sufficiently explained in your textbook; to appreciate nuances, recognize differences of opinion, follow arguments, understand conclusions, and so learn more than would otherwise have been possible. Going over things again should help to clear up any misunderstandings and to fix important points in your mind. You should also be well placed to ask questions if anything remains unclear.

The lecturer should neither teach the subject, in the sense of telling you all that you need to know, nor provide a summary of your textbook. The lecturer should:

1. Guide your thoughts.
2. Indicate the scope of the subject.
3. Provide a level of treatment that is appropriate to your needs.
4. Emphasize basic essentials.
5. Explain difficult points.
6. Clarify aspects that are commonly misunderstood.
7. Give evidence and examples.
8. Draw attention to different interpretations of the evidence.
9. Relate new work to your previous knowledge and experience.
10. Suggest sources of further information and ideas.
11. Stimulate your thinking.
12. Help you to develop a critical interest in the subject.
13. Answer your questions.

In lectures it is best to sit in the middle and near the front, with other keen students, where you are close to the lecturer, can hear all that is said, see the blackboard and any other visual aids clearly, and feel closely involved. In this position you will not be distracted by other students, sitting between you and the lecturer.

MAKE GOOD NOTES DURING LECTURES

In a lecture to a large number of students, a lecturer may neither ask questions nor wish to answer questions – except at the end. However, communication should not be one way: as a student you should not be passive. You are participating in a group activity. A good lecturer, who is sensitive to the needs and reactions of the audience, will look around the room and try to maintain eye contact with everyone. You can help by looking at the lecturer and, by your facial expression, *showing that you are interested* and that you do or do not understand. If necessary, the lecturer will respond by repeating, by putting things in a different way, or by summarizing – in an attempt to ensure that your attention is maintained and that you do understand.

The worst lectures are those in which the lecturer reads notes and most students try to record every word: the lecturer's notes are transferred to the notepaper of the students. The students have difficulty in keeping up, are likely to make mistakes, and nobody has time to think. Alternatively, the bad lecturer copies on the blackboard things such as proofs and classical derivations which are written out in full in the textbooks for the course. Again, most students are so busy recording that they are unable to concentrate on the argument. As a result, they miss important comments and necessary explanations and are unable to understand. They are not ready to ask questions either during the argument, when something is not clear, or at the end when things are still not clear.

A good lecturer provides a list of titles, with the date of each lecture, at the start of the lecture course; then writes a title on the blackboard at the start of each lecture. The purpose of the lecture should be clear from the title and from the lecturer's introductory remarks. You should be able to see how one lecture follows on from previous lectures and is leading to the next. Is the lecturer explaining different points of view, introducing new ideas, adding information, presenting evidence, or drawing conclusions?

You should be aware of the lecturer's purpose and should be listening, thinking and anticipating. You should be relating what is being said to what you already know, and selecting points so that your notes are a digest. Instead of *taking notes* dictated by the lecturer, you should be listening, selecting and *making your own notes*. The lecturer may help you to select and record the main points by writing headings and key words on a blackboard, by repetition, a change of voice, a meaningful pause, or by using such phrases as: *most important, note that,* and *remember that,* to emphasise things that you may wish to record. Words such as *first, second, also, furthermore, moreover, therefore,* and *finally,* indicate stages in an argument. *But* and *however* indicate a qualification. *Because* indicates a reason. *On the one hand* and *on the other hand* indicate a contrast. *Illustrated by, for example,* and *as seen in,* all indicate an example. All these words, although you may not record them, help you to make good notes.

Lecture notes are so important as a record of the course content, and as a basis for further studies and for revision, that you must try to make good notes from the start of any course. If you looked at the notes taken by students who had attended a lecture, you would find that they had all selected different points for inclusion and arranged them in different ways. This is as it should be. There is no one correct method for making notes. However, consider the following suggestions.

You have to look down from time to time to make brief notes but

Table 5.1 Some useful abbreviations and symbols

Abbreviation	Meaning	Symbol	Meaning
N.B.	note particularly	mm	millimetre(s)
cf.	compare	cm	centimetre(s)
ct.	contrast	m	metre(s)
e.g.	for example	km	kilometre(s)
i.e.	that is	ha	hectare(s)
no.	number	cm^3	cubic centimetre(s)
p.	page	l	litre(s)
pp.	pages	kg	kilogramme(s)
ch.	chapter	t	tonne(s)
ed.	edition or editor	s	second(s)
w/o	without	min	minute(s)
fig.	figure (diagram)	h	hour(s)
ref.	reference	°C	degree Celsius
C19	19th century	%	per cent
L.	Latin	+	and or plus
Gk.	Greek	=	equal to
vol.	volume	≠	different from
conc.	concentrated	<	less than
aq.	aqueous	>	greater than

try not to write non-stop. You can make note-taking easier by using well-known abbreviations and symbols (see Table 5.1) and, for example, by using capital initial letters instead of proper names – if this can be done without causing confusion. However, use abbreviations so that you can spend more time on listening, thinking, and selecting, not so that you can make more notes.

To record every word of every lecture, if this could be done, in shorthand for example, would be a waste of time.

1. You would not be able to take a critical interest in the lectures.
2. You would not be trying to understand and learn.
3. You would not be ready to ask questions at the end of each lecture.
4. You would have a record that was too long to be of use in your further studies.
5. You would have to read through this record, later, to pick out the essentials of each lecture, so that you could *make your own notes*. To make notes it is necessary to be selective; and you are advised to select at the first opportunity (in the lecture). You do not have time to do everything twice.

Sequential notes

Record first the title of the lecture, the name of the lecturer, and the date. Listen carefully and record all the main points in the order in which they are made during the lecture. Record:

1. A numbered list of main points.
2. Concise summaries of the supporting detail.
3. Examples.
4. Simple diagrams (e.g. Fig. 5.3).
5. Dates and numbers (if possible in a table, see p. 53).
6. Enough explanation to provide continuity.
7. Any new words.
8. All quotations, definitions, and summaries, dictated by the lecturer.
9. Details of any sources of information mentioned in the lecture (see p. 48).

Notes arranged in this way, preserving the order decided upon by the lecturer, and including all stages in any argument, are called linear or sequential notes. Such notes help you to recollect what was said in the lecture and any relevant discussion.

Remember that visual aids used in the lecture are not intended for your entertainment. They are part of the lecture and appropriate notes should be made. A good lecturer will not talk whilst writing or drawing and will give you time to study a completed diagram or visual aid before starting any explanation.

During the lecture, mark anything that you do not understand. For example, put a vertical line and a question mark in the margin. You can then ask a question at the end of the lecture or try to find the answer yourself before the next lecture.

Start each topic on a new sheet of notepaper and write on one side of each sheet only. You can then add sheets in the most appropriate places when you work on your notes later. Also, leave wide margins and plenty of space between lines of writing – for corrections and additions (see Fig. 5.2).

Creative pattern notes

An alternative, sometimes called the creative pattern method, is not sequential. The lecture title is written in the centre of a page, inside a

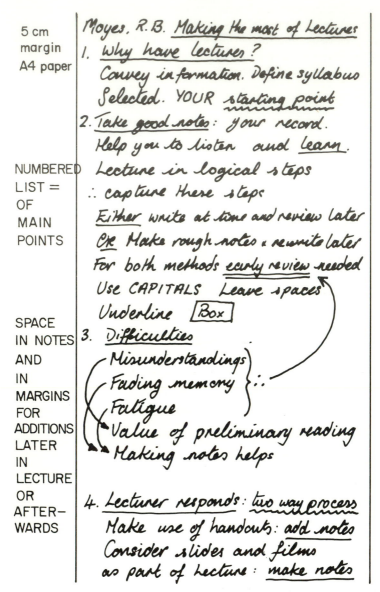

Fig. 5.2 Notes made in a lecture. This lecture by Dr R. B. Moyes is included in Haynes, L. J. (ed.) (1977) *Effective Learning: a practical guide for students*, Tape recording and booklet, Tetradon Publications, Guildford, England.

circle, and then radiating lines are added to link this *central idea* to the topics covered in the lecture. Each topic is written as one or a few words (headings) and further lines radiate from each of these headings – pointing to supporting details each of which is noted as one key word or phrase. The result is a diagram (similar to Fig. 6.3, p. 67).

This method has the advantage that it makes the student listen to the lecture, concentrating not only on each main point but also on considering how these fit in to the picture as a whole. But these things can be done by students who use the sequential method, who should also be recognizing topics and selecting appropriate sub-headings. Moreover, creative pattern notes have the following disadvantages.

1. The notes made, irrespective of the content of the lecture, are restricted to one page – unless a separate diagram is prepared for each topic covered in the lecture.
2. The notes must be restricted to key words or phrases. There is no space for whole sentences (e.g. definitions) or for complete bibliographic references, unless these are written on separate sheets, so that the student has to prepare creative pattern and sequential notes at the same time.
3. There is no space for corrections or additions in later study periods. For this reason, and also because the notes must be very rough, more work is needed after the lecture to produce another neater set of notes.
4. The student, looking at the notes later, cannot recapture the lecturer's train of thought. The plan of the lecture (topic outline) is lost in creating a non-sequential diagram.
5. A non-sequential record is unsuitable in some subjects (including mathematics and most engineering and science subjects) in which the logical development of an argument or proof must be recorded.

Other kinds of notes

You will find it helpful to use different methods of note-making on different occasions – for different lectures and even for the parts of one lecture – depending upon your purpose and the way the material is presented for your consideration.

The notes taken in a lecture may be set out as a table (see Table 5.2)

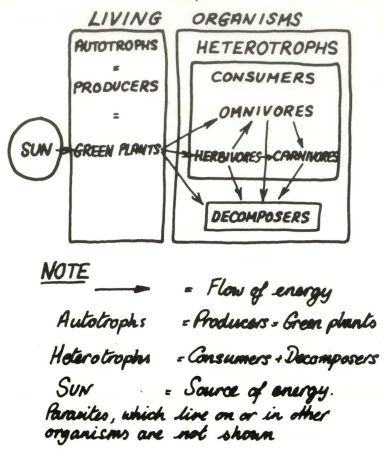

Fig. 5.3   Lecture notes made as a diagram with annotations.

or as a diagram (see Fig. 5.3), with annotations, to provide a convenient summary.

Also look at the notes made by other students during a lecture and compare them with your own. Are they about the same length as yours, and arranged in a similar way? Can you learn anything about note-making from them?

To give yourself practice in listening and selecting, and making notes, all at the same time, listen to a recorded talk. Make notes during the talk (see Fig. 5.2); then play the recording again to check that you have noted the main points.

To make selection easier in class, do some preliminary reading. You can then concentrate on listening, picking out the main points (the things your lecturer considers important), understanding, noting, and appreciating the lecturer's approach.

Get into the habit of asking good questions

At the end of a lecture, *if you have not already been told*, (i) ask for the lecturer's name, and (ii) ask what the next lecture will be about, and (iii) ask for a list of lecture titles, with dates, and suggestions for preliminary reading.

If there is time for questions or discussion during or at the end of a class, take the opportunity to ask for further explanation of anything that was not immediately clear. You are unlikely to be the only one who did not understand. Your questions will therefore help others and will encourage them to ask questions; and you should learn from all the lecturer's replies.

Questions not only help students to learn but also indicate interest in the subject, and this makes the lecturer's work more rewarding. Furthermore, questions should help the lecturer first to recognize things that students find difficult and then to give better lectures. More questions will come to mind during your further studies. Try to find the answers, before the next lecture (see Fig. 5.4), in the ways discussed in Chapters 7 and 8. This will help you to learn.

Your success in filling gaps in your knowledge, by finding the answers to your own questions, will also help you to gain confidence as a student and will provide the basic understanding needed for further progress. You will also be encouraged, by your own efforts, to further effective study. However, there will be times when you do not find the information you need. You may also come across contradictions and then not know whom or what to believe. You should then ask good questions. You will find that some lecturers encourage questions and discussion during or at the end of each class. Others prefer to give individual help in tutorials.

Do not be afraid to go to see a lecturer to clear up any difficult point or to seek further guidance. If you choose an appropriate place and time most lecturers will welcome your interest in their subject. You should therefore get to know the special interests of all your lecturers so that when you have a problem you will know who to consult. Go prepared, with your questions and notes or a textbook, so that you can pinpoint your difficulty and get help quickly.

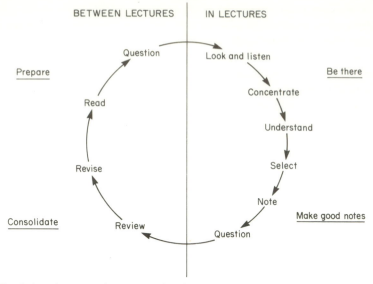

Fig. 5.4   Aspects of active study: things to do before, during and after a lecture, tutorial or seminar.

AFTER THE LECTURE

A good lecturer will make your work easier, and more interesting, but you still have to do the work. The notes taken in a lecture provide a foundation upon which your knowledge can be built. They are not all that you need to know but they should provide a basis for further work. Thinking again about a lecture, *while it is fresh in your mind*, helps you to recall the lecture and is an aid to active study (see p. 61).

Review

As soon as possible after the lecture, preferably on the same evening, review your notes to make sure that you understand them now and that you will be able to understand them later. Check that they are an accurate record, containing the most important points and enough supporting detail.

   Do your best to master each subject (especially fundamentals) as you go along. Your early work is a basis for later work and so for progress on the course. Make a note of any questions that need to be answered or of any points that you do not fully understand. These are tasks for later study sessions (see p. 32).

Checking your notes and adding to them, where necessary, will help you to recall much of what was said in the lecture, will increase your understanding, and will help you to learn and to remember. However, do not get into the time-wasting habit of copying out notes neatly. If you are thinking during lectures and selecting carefully, you should be able to write legibly. If the lecture has been well organized (and if you made sequential notes, see p. 47), you should have arranged your notes neatly, during the lecture, in a well organized sequence – similar to the topic outline prepared by the lecturer when he was deciding what to say. You should have brief notes that will be useful for both quick reference and revision. If the lecture has not been well planned, or if the lecturer has tried to say too much in the time available, you may not have been able to make good notes during the lecture: you will need to do more work on your notes while the lecture is fresh on your mind.

When you are satisfied with your notes on a lecture, mark the most important points, for emphasis, by numbering, underlining, or boxing (see Fig. 5.2). Then look back at the previous lecture and at earlier lectures in the series, so that you can refresh your memory, review your progress, and see how the course is developing.

Table 5.2 Lecture notes made as a table with annotations*

World Regions	1970			2000†	
	Cultivated area (millions of hectares)	Population estimate (millions)	Cultivated area per person (hectares)	Population forecast (millions)	Cultivated area per person (hectares)
Africa	165	345	0.48	750	0.22
Asia	475	2055	0.23	4090	0.12
Australia and New Zealand	20	20	1.00	35	0.57
Europe	150	460	0.33	580	0.26
North America	240	320	0.75	530	0.45
South America	80	190	0.42	440	0.18
USSR	230	245	0.94	340	0.68

* To prevent mistakes in copying, notes of this kind are best provided as a hand-out by the lecturer.
† Calculation of cultivated area per person in 2000 based on expected population growth and the assumption that the loss of cultivated land due to soil erosion and urbanization can be offset by bringing marginal lands into cultivation.

Study any hand-out supplied during the lecture. It may provide a summary of the main points made in the lecture (see Table 5.2), a diagram, or additions to what was said in the lecture. A lecturer who prepares a hand-out thinks it will be useful to you. Therefore, it should either be read and then filed with your lecture notes, or material extracted from it should be incorporated in your lecture notes. If you throw even one hand-out away, without reading it, or if you file it in the wrong place, you may find that you are unable to answer a question set by this lecturer in one of your examinations.

Revise

Your review of a lecture, which should take perhaps twenty minutes, should be followed by about ten minutes of revision. From memory, list the most important points or basic essentials and write out any definitions. Then check to see that you have remembered correctly. This short time spent on revision will help to fix in your mind those things that you wish to remember (see p. 61). Before the next lecture, if you can, look at the sources of further information mentioned in this lecture.

GET THE MOST OUT OF TUTORIALS AND SEMINARS

Tutorials

In some tutorials you may have the opportunity to discuss home-work with your tutor, after it has been marked. Alternatively, a few students may meet regularly as a tutorial group *to discuss a previously arranged topic*.

In a tutorial, because you are not starting something new, you should be well prepared. You should have looked at the syllabus and at your lecture notes on this and related topics. Perhaps you will have had time for some background reading. You should therefore be ready to participate in the discussion, to answer questions, and to ask questions – so that you can try to clear up any difficulties or seek advice on, for example, suitable background reading or sources of further information on particular points.

The best preparation for a tutorial is probably to think about the topic that is to be discussed, as if you were preparing to write about it (see Chapter 6). You may then take to the tutorial:

1. A topic outline (see p. 105).
2. A list of questions.
3. Your lecture notes on this subject.

These will help you to take an active part in the discussion and to keep each of your contributions short and to the point (Fig. 5.5). In a tutorial develop your ability to listen to, and to learn from, all contributions. Take these opportunities to evaluate, to discuss, to ask for clarification, and to ask other questions.

A tutor usually introduces the topic for discussion and encourages all those present to participate, whilst discouraging long contributions and digressions. The tutor may also comment or ask questions at appropriate points, to help the discussion along, and towards the end may indicate any omissions, sum up, and try to come to some conclusion.

SIT IN A CIRCLE SO THAT YOU CAN SEE EVERYONE

Fig. 5.5 Be prepared to participate in discussions, but do not talk for too long.

In tutorials do not hesitate to contribute. Take these opportunities to gain confidence in speaking about your subjects, and to develop your abilities to make your meaning clear, to argue logically and tactfully, to listen to different points of view, to question, to make considered criticisms and comments, and to express your opinions and state the evidence upon which they are based. As you learn more about how to contribute effectively to a discussion, you are developing your abilities to speak, think, and learn, about your subjects.

Participating in discussions, trying to explain something, and listening to different interpretations of the evidence, are all activities that make you think about your subjects and organize your thoughts. Such discussions should be interesting and stimulating. Going over things in your mind, and in conversation – in tutorials and other discussions – makes you reconsider aspects of your work and so helps you to remember important points. During a tutorial you can make notes and amend your topic outline.

Because discussion is an aid to thinking, understanding, learning, and remembering, the members of a tutorial group may arrange meetings, without their tutor, so that they have further opportunities to benefit from group study. In addition, all students should take other opportunities for informal discussion so that they can help one another.

Seminars

More people are present at a seminar than at a tutorial, and one student may have been asked to introduce the topic that is to be

Table 5.3 Preparing for a discussion

Stages in preparation	Activities
Think	*List* relevant points. *Prepare* first draft of a topic outline.
Plan	*Note* difficulties encountered, gaps in your knowledge, and questions. Consult your own notes and references cited in lectures. Try to clear up difficulties, fill gaps, and answer questions or solve problems.
Write	*Revise* your topic outline. *Number* points you consider should be made in the discussion. *List* questions you would like to ask.
	Listen to the discussion. *Contribute*. State opinions and evidence. Explain. Ask questions. *Make notes*
Revise	After the discussion *review* your lecture notes on the subject and *revise* them if necessary.

discussed. All those present should have had the opportunity to consider the topic and, as for a tutorial, they should be well prepared and ready to participate in the discussion.

The first speaker should base a brief introduction, lasting up to ten minutes, on a topic outline – and should draw attention to one or two points which are topical or which, for some other reason, merit special attention at this seminar. All contributions to the discussion, and all questions and answers, should be brief and to the point, so that everyone can have an opportunity to speak. As with tutorials, use seminars as opportunities to learn. Take part in the discussion (see Fig. 5.5). Listen to other contributors. Make concise notes. After tutorials or seminars consider what you have learned and amend your lecture notes, so that all your notes on each topic will be in one place (see p. 89). See also Table 5.3.

WRITING PAPER AND STORAGE MATERIALS

Writing paper

At the start of your course of study, consider carefully what materials you will require. However, you are advised not to buy these before the course starts because you may be given definite instructions about the writing materials to be used for course work. It is also best to seek the advice of your lecturers before purchasing any special equipment that may be needed for your course (e.g. drawing instruments and calculators).

Wide-lined A4 paper (29.5 x 21 cm) with a 2.5 cm margin is provided in most examinations, and it is a good idea to use this kind of paper for all your written work, unless you are instructed to do otherwise. Narrow-lined paper is a false economy – because, for written work, there is no space between the lines for minor additions or for a marker's comments and corrections. The cost of paper is small, compared with the cost of your education, and it is worth giving yourself space in which to work.

It is probably best to carry enough loose-leaf paper for one day's notes (in an envelope or folder), and to write on one side of each page only, so that the notes made during the day can be transferred to appropriate files, kept at home, each evening. This reduces the chances of losing all your notes on a subject. Also, pages can be inserted, rearranged or removed, easily, whenever necessary. Bound notebooks, which are useful to a pupil at school for notes dictated by a teacher, are not recommended for students who are making their own notes.

Storing information

Your notes are for use, not for permanent storage. They are the basis for active study: not a graveyard in which ideas can rest in peace. They should be readily available for consultation, for regular use in revision, and for the addition of ideas, information and examples.

If you use loose-leaf paper, as recommended, your notes on each subject may be stored at home. Keep them either in A4 envelopes that will accept the paper without folding, or in a clearly labelled manilla folder. Store the envelopes in box files or, as a cheap alternative, in large cereal packets from which one side or one end has been removed. If you prefer to use folders, light-weight manilla folders with cords (not rings) are probably best. Ring-binders are bulky even when empty and they do not hold the paper firmly.

Index cards (or postcards) are useful. Use a separate card for a complete bibliographic record (see p. 48) of each source of information that you have found useful, so that you can consult the same source again if necessary. You may also find index cards useful when you prepare your own revision aids (see p. 145). Small cards (125 × 75 mm) are large enough for most purposes and they can be stored in a cardboard shoe box.

There is no need, as a student, for you to spend money on expensive hard-backed folders, box files, or filing drawers. Your money is better spent on writing paper and necessary reference books.

6

Think – organize – select – remember

A philatelist may remember every stamp in a large collection, and a card player the order in which all cards were played in a game. Similarly, you can remember interesting things. To master a new subject you need only to start at the beginning, have a desire to learn, take an active interest, and use effective study techniques.

ORGANIZE AND SELECT

This is the sequence in effective study:

1. Select things to record as you observe, listen, or read.
2. Review your notes to make sure that you do understand them and that they are well organized.
3. Recognize the fundamentals and select other important points that you wish to remember.
4. Mark these things for emphasis – so that they stand out from the supporting detail when you . . .
5. Revise and try to remember.

There is no point in trying to remember things that you do not understand; and you would have great difficulty if you tried to learn pages of notes parrot-fashion. Also, such rote learning is usually a waste of time because most questions set in course work and examinations call for understanding as well as knowledge.

In marking it is easy to distinguish passages that a student has copied from a textbook, or remembered from lecture notes, without understanding. Few marks can be given for the display of knowledge that you have not made your own (see plagiarism, p. 102); and examination *howlers* or *boners* are blunders that occur when students try to write about half-remembered things that they do not understand.

HOW TO REMEMBER

1. Pay attention when new topics are introduced in class, or as you are reading. *First impressions make a great impact.* A good lecturer or author can help you to learn by making your first experience of each topic accurate, understandable, and interesting. Similarly, you can help yourself by concentrating and getting things right the first time.
2. Shortly after learning something you may remember most of it, but as time goes by you may forget more and more. Therefore, revise each topic soon after you learn it (see Table 6.1) and then *keep each aspect of your work fresh in your mind.*
3. Learning is aided by concentrating on *one task at a time.* This is why half an hour of active study is better than a longer period of half-hearted or poorly directed effort.
4. *Learning and remembering are aided by association.* It helps you to remember if each new thought can be linked to things you already know, or if things you wish to learn can be arranged in a pattern or diagram.
5. *Learning is aided by the use of different senses*: by seeing, hearing and writing in lectures; and by seeing and touching in practical work. Learning is helped if you can confirm or find things out for yourself.
6. *Learning is easiest if things give you pleasure.* Pleasure may come from listening to an enthusiastic teacher, from reading a good book, from increased knowledge and understanding, and from good marks awarded or praise received.
7. *Learning and remembering are aided by repetition.* Some students find their work easy but have difficulty in remembering. Others have initial difficulties but then retain the knowledge. This is probably because, in trying to understand, they have had to think about the work again and again.

Table 6.1 Repetition as part of active study

Activity	Time	Spacing your revision
1. Preliminary reading	Day before class	— 12 hours
2. Listen	In class	
3. Make notes		
4. Discuss		— 6 hours
5. Check notes	Same evening	— 4 days
6. Review and revise	Next weekend	— 4 days
7. Revise	When you review next lecture	— 6 weeks
8. Review	Each time you use your knowledge	— ? ?
9. Revise	Next vacation	— 12 weeks
	Next vacation	— 6 weeks
10. Revise	Before examination	

Repetition helps to fix things in your mind. You may remember more, therefore, if you read something twice quickly in preference to once slowly (see also p. 83). Similarly, whatever you wish to learn and remember, you will probably find it most effective to devote several short study periods to the task rather than a single long one. In the later periods you add to what you have already absorbed; this method of learning things for the first time (little by little) incorporates the beneficial effects of revision. This is another reason for breaking longer study sessions into shorter periods of active study (see p. 38).

Revise regularly

Revision should be a regular part of active study. At the start of every study period it is a good idea to spend two minutes thinking about how the work fits into your previous studies. Also, end every study period with a few minutes devoted to a review and to revision;

consider what you have achieved or learned and, if appropriate, list
the main points as a concise summary.

On the following weekend, or as soon as possible after learning
something for the first time, work on your notes again. Check again
that you understand. If you have not already done so, mark important points (see p. 53) and add examples as an aid to remembering.
Make sure that the things you wish to remember are in an order that
suits your purpose.

What you already know provides an organized basis for further
work. You must, therefore, master your subject step by step.
Without a grasp of the fundamentals you will have no basis for
understanding the more advanced work – just as if you miss one
lecture you may not understand the next (see Fig. 5.1, p. 42).

Study each topic again and again: by preliminary reading; by
attending lectures and other organized classes; by checking and
reviewing your notes; by revising on the following week-end; when
reviewing your later lectures in the same series; each time you
use your knowledge of the subject (e.g. in preparing topic outlines
and summaries); in each vacation; and before examinations (see
Table 6.1).

Working on your notes helps you to recall what was said in a
lecture (or what you have read or observed). You see the most
important points emphasised. You see diagrams. You review your
progress and see each topic as part of a whole. You recognize your
weaknesses and can work on them. You identify key concepts and
make connections between topics and subjects. You understand
more and more. Regular revision, therefore, is an essential part of
active study. Good students attend to each subject regularly and not
just in a last desperate attempt to learn things for the first time in the
weeks before an examination.

Learn some things by heart

People of any age can fix things in their minds by repeating them
aloud once a day for about a week. This is the way to learn new
words, spelling, short quotations, poems, definitions, laws, rules,
important dates, multiplication tables, formulae, symbols, and
similar fundamentals of your subject. See also revision notes, p. 145.

If things you must remember can be said as a rhyme, or with a
certain rhythm, it is easy to say them again and again until they

cannot be forgotten. For example, in spelling:

> When the sound is ee
> Remember
> i before e
> except after c.

And in different languages there are rhymes to help children remember how many days there are in each month.

> Thirty days hath September,
> April, June and November.
> All the rest have thirty one,
> Except February with twenty eight.
> And, once in four,
> February shall have one day more.

Some people find it helpful to remember a memory cue or mnemonic. For example, the initial letters of the sentence 'Richard of York Gave Battle in Vain' should help you to recall the order of colours in a spectrum: Red, Orange, Yellow, Green, Blue, Indigo, and Violet. However, learning too many mnemonics could lead to confusion – making it harder to remember instead of easier.

USE YOUR KNOWLEDGE

When you learn a language, it is easiest to remember new words if you use them regularly in appropriate contexts. Similarly, whatever you study, try to use all your knowledge of each subject at every appropriate opportunity (see Fig. 6.4).

1. Consider any practical applications of each aspect of your work.
2. When you have a question to answer in course work or in examinations, consider all aspects of your work (see p. 65), so that you can recall relevant material and select from all that you know.
3. Set yourself questions as a test (see p. 147) so that you can use your newly acquired knowledge, draw upon different aspects of your work as an aid to revision, and practice writing a good answer in the time that would be available in an examination.
4. Construct flow charts and other diagrams (like Fig. 5.3) that will help you to organize your thoughts, contribute to your

*TRY TO EXPLAIN SOMETHING
SIMPLY TO A FRIEND*

Fig. 6.1   Before you can explain anything you must understand it yourself.

understanding, and be useful as revision aids. Many things can be represented diagramatically and you may find it easier to visualize diagrams than to remember words alone.

5. Write out things that you must remember, from memory, and then check that they are correct. Using your knowledge in this way should be a regular part of your revision.

6. When you think you understand something, try to explain it simply to a friend (see Fig. 6.1). Alternatively, try to explain it to yourself, in writing, and then check your own work. Either way, you will have to arrange your thoughts and confirm that you do understand. Then you can make a note of any new insights – or of the need for further work.

Plan answers to questions

Thinking about questions and planning answers, as well as being a preparation for writing (see p. 105), is a method of active study (see Fig. 9.3, p. 104) that helps you:

1. To distinguish main points from supporting detail.
2. To select the most appropriate examples.
3. To develop an ability to select only relevant material and, therefore, to reject anything that is irrelevant.

4. To organize relevant information and ideas.
5. To recognize gaps in your knowledge.

Think. When you are sure what the question means (see p. 121), make a note of any terms in the question. In your answer you must make clear that you understand their meaning, either by defining them or by using them correctly in appropriate contexts.

Consider carefully what is needed for a complete answer to the question asked. Write words and phrases, spread over a whole page, as you think about the main parts of your answer (see Fig. 6.2). These will serve as subheadings, below which you can add further notes as you think of relevant information, examples and ideas that might be included in each part.

Some people prefer to record their thoughts in a diagram (see Fig. 6.3). You will find which way suits you best: in both you can distinguish main points from supporting detail or examples, and arrows can be used to indicate possible connections — which may help you to decide upon an effective order for your paragraphs.

To stimulate your thoughts, ask yourself the six questions that children use when they want to know something. Remember:

> There are six honest serving men,
> Who taught me all I knew.
> They are: What? Where? and When?
> And How? and Why? and Who?

Your answers to these questions can never be just yes or no (see Fig. 4.3, p. 35).

Another recall technique is to consider the different aspects of your subject, or to wonder how a question would be tackled by specialists in different branches of your subject, or by people with differing points of view. Such thoughts may help you to bring together topics that are relevant to your answer, but which did not immediately come to mind when you first read the question.

Plan. Work on your preliminary notes, prepared as you thought about the question. Add numbers (see Figs 6.2 and 6.3) as you decide:

1. How your answer is to be introduced.
2., 3., 4., 5. . . . What the topic for each paragraph is to be, and . . .
6. How your answer is to be drawn to an effective conclusion.

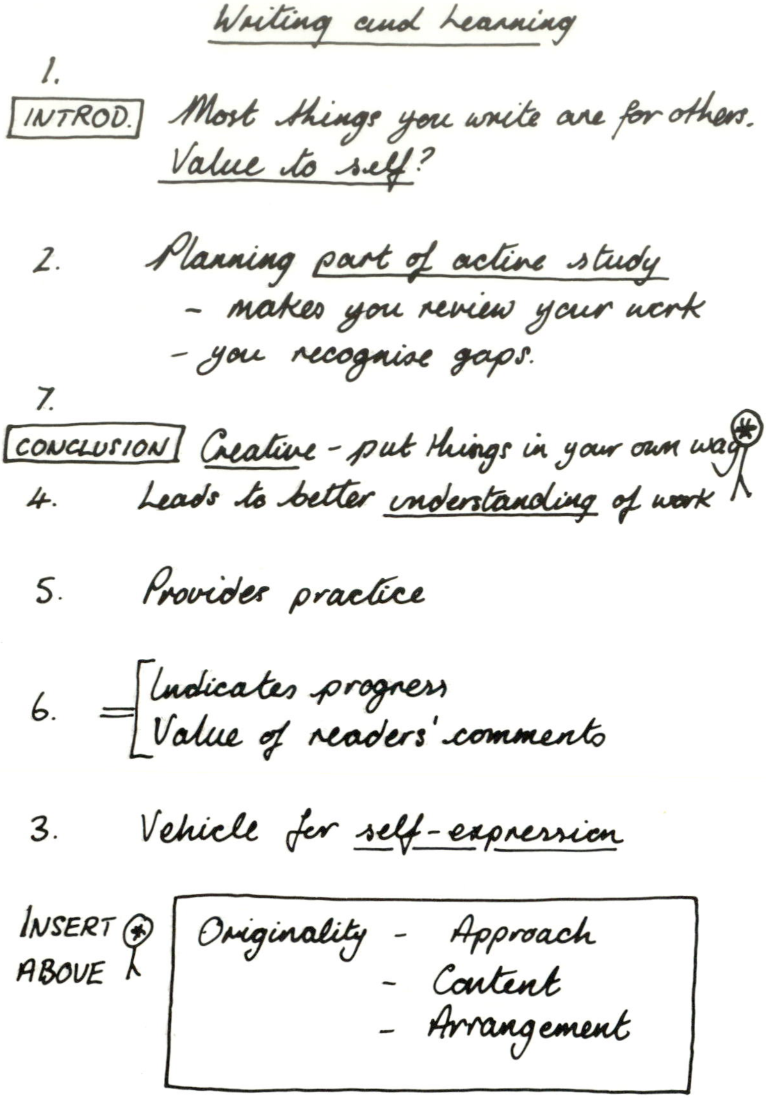

<u>Writing and Learning</u>

1.

| INTROD. | Most things you write are for others. <u>Value to self?</u>

2. Planning <u>part of active study</u>
    – makes you review your work
    – you recognise gaps.

7.

| CONCLUSION | Creative – put things in your own way ✱

4. Leads to better <u>understanding</u> of work ↖

5. Provides practice

6. ⎡Indicates progress
    ⎣Value of readers' comments

3. Vehicle for <u>self-expression</u>

INSERT ✱
ABOVE ↖
| Originality – Approach
    – Content
    – Arrangement |

Fig. 6.2 First thoughts for a composition on the importance of writing in study, with numbers added after further thought – to indicate the order of paragraphs in a topic outline or plan.

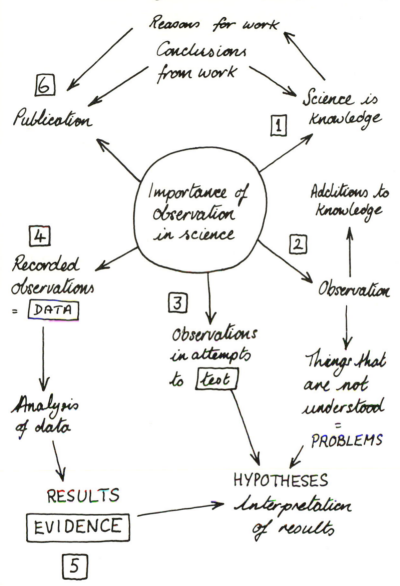

Fig. 6.3 First thoughts for a composition on the importance of observation in science, with numbers added after further thought – to indicate the order of paragraphs in a topic outline or plan.

After even a few minutes of thought and reflection you may have decided on the main parts of your answer and made a note of many points that could be included in each part. Indeed, because planning is itself a stimulus to thinking, you will usually find that *you know more about the subject than you at first realized*.

In an examination you may be able to spare only a few minutes for preliminary thoughts and for planning your answer. In course work you have more time but your first step should still be to think about the question and make concise notes of things that should be in your answer. Always do this before looking at your lecture notes or at other sources of information, so that you can: *ensure a fresh approach*; consider which aspects of your work may be relevant; test your memory and understanding; and recognize where further information is needed. This is also good practice for examinations in which you must rely on what you know.

Having prepared a plan, look at your lecture notes or at other sources of information (see Chapters 7 and 8) so that you can fill any gaps, learn more about your subject, and then give a more complete answer to the question asked (see p. 156).

EXERCISE YOUR MIND

The techniques for thinking, understanding and remembering, recommended in this chapter involve the regular revision of all subjects, and of all parts of each subject. Regular revision, learning by heart, and using your knowledge in conversation and writing, all make you think about your work repeatedly (see Fig. 6.4). This helps you to understand, to see connections, and to remember.

We all forget things in which we are not interested – because we rarely think about them. Good students, however, attend to each subject regularly (see p. 61). This does not mean that they have to do more work than other students. On the contrary, they avoid last minute cramming and make their work easier:

1. By spreading the load.
2. Because each time they revise it is easier to refresh the memory than the time before.
3. Because each time they revise they see connections between recent work and their earlier studies.

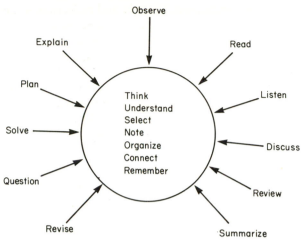

Fig. 6.4 Acquiring and using knowledge: activities in study that contribute to learning.

7

Find out for yourself

Thinking and planning enable you to set down what you know and to recognize gaps in your knowledge. Your purpose in study should then be to fill these gaps, so that you can understand each subject better and give more complete answers to questions.

In all subjects which bear upon everyday experience there are many things that you can find out for yourself. In many ways this is the best way to learn: you are likely to remember things that you have seen and noted (but see Fig. 7.1). In practical work in a laboratory, studio or workshop, therefore, it is not enough to follow

YOU ARE LIKELY TO REMEMBER THINGS YOU HAVE SEEN FOR YOURSELF

Fig. 7.1 A student, like anyone else, has a limited ability to maintain attention and make complete and accurate observations.

instructions. You must think about your work; use your knowledge; confirm things that you have been told or read; use these opportunities to learn. For the same reasons, approach field work, organized visits, and opportunities to travel, with enthusiasm. By observation you can broaden and extend your experience. Also, in all these activities a supervisor will be present to answer your questions, discuss any problems, and help in other ways.

DIFFICULTIES IN THE WAY OF ACCURATE OBSERVATION

You may regard things you have seen as facts, but observation is not easy. The following are some reasons why observers make incomplete and inaccurate observations.

(a) Inadequate preparation

Satisfactory practical work depends upon adequate preparation.

Self. You must know what you are doing and why it is worthwhile. You should be in the right state of mind. This is why practical exercises usually follow lectures on the subject or, in project work, they follow background reading, a literature survey, or preliminary observations.

Equipment. Many instruments are used as aids to observation. They extend your ability to observe (e.g. telescopes and oscilloscopes) or to make precise measurements (e.g. rulers and thermometers), but you must know how to use any equipment and how to check that it is working properly.

Materials. In science subjects all glassware, for example, must be clean, and all chemicals must be pure.

Methods. The procedure to be followed must be clearly stated. This is why a practical schedule is usually provided for each class.

Such preparations are necessary so that a clear statement can be made of the conditions under which observations were made; so that the observations recorded are accurate (i.e. can be regarded as data); and so that, if necessary, similar observations can be made again under similar conditions.

(b) Lack of concentration throughout an observation

A break in attention may be due to distraction, to the need to look
away to use an instrument or make a note, or to fatigue. A definite
and sustained effort is needed if you are to miss nothing. This is why
preparing an accurate drawing or diagram, which makes you look
carefully, is an aid to complete and accurate description. In describing an object or scene it is necessary to look at each part separately, to
make sure that you see details as well as the whole.

> His eyes seemed hooded in the shadow of the hat's brim. He
> came closer, and I could see that this was because the brows were
> drawn in a frown of fixed and habitual alertness. Beneath them
> the eyes were endlessly searching from side to side and forward,
> checking off every item in view, missing nothing.
>
> *Shane*, Jack Schaeffer (1954)

(c) Abstraction

In everyday life you ignore many things. Life would be unbearable
without such abstraction, but the result is that you may disregard
things which later assume some importance. In making observations, be aware of this difficulty that stands in the way of complete
and accurate description.

> Mr Mockridge was 'so commonplace a figure to Jeremy that, on
> ordinary days, he was shrouded by an invisibility of tradition.'
>
> *Jeremy*, Hugh Walpole (1919)

(d) Inexperience

When you look at anything for the first time, you are like an explorer
venturing into the unknown. The difficulty of seeing all, or indeed of
seeing anything, when there is so much to see, and you do not know
what to look for, is well illustrated by a child's view of the inside of a
gypsy's caravan, as he imagined it would be:

> There would be so many things to see that it would be hard to
> distinguish separate objects.
>
> *Thrush Green*, 'Miss Read' (1959)

(e) Experience

Although preparation is necessary, reading before you investigate may direct your mind along well worn tracks and away from a fresh approach to a problem. Knowing what to expect may also be a barrier to complete and accurate observation.

> It is that which we do know which is the greatest hindrance to our learning, not that which we do not know.
>
> Claude Bernard (1813–1878)

Taking things for granted. Many things happen with such regularity that you may come to accept that they always happen. There may then be occasions when you are prepared to believe that something has happened when it has not.

Seeing only the expected. When you observe an event, with many things happening together, you may see only some of these things – even if you observe the same sequence many times (as in a film). You may have had the experience, if you have seen a film more than once, of seeing more in your second and third observations of the same events. Perhaps certain things captured your attention: these may have been the things that you expected to see. Because it is sometimes difficult to see more than expected, and so add to observations, it may be difficult to make original observations.

> For several years (1926 to 1932) the tracks of positrons in cloud-chamber photographs [of cosmic rays] were either ignored or attributed to dirt, until Anderson and Blackett [independently] appreciated their significance [in 1932]. Yet the existence of these particles had been predicted by Dirac in 1930.
>
> *The Concept of the Positron*, N.R. Hanson (1963)

Seeing only the unexpected. Sometimes you may fail to see familiar things, that are expected, because your attention has been captured by something that does not usually happen, or that has gone unnoticed previously. Your record of the observation may then be incomplete – because only the unexpected event can be adequately recorded.

Stuck in a groove. By making observations in the same way, day after day, you may record useful data. But what you see will be limited by the method used. Because of this fixed routine, you may be less likely to break new ground than would be someone coming new to the project who looked at things in a new way.

Previous experience. In 1928 Alexander Fleming was interested in the bactericidal properties of natural secretions, such as tears. His later observation that no bacteria were growing in the part of a culture medium contaminated by the fungus *Penicillium*, was the first step that lead to the discovery and isolation of the antibiotic penicillin. Because the contamination of the culture was not planned, the observation of the effect of the contaminant was made possible by an accident, yet Fleming's mind was prepared by his previous experience: he considered the possible importance of an observation that another scientist might have ignored.

In science most discoveries are made by accident in experiments designed for other purposes – but they are made by scientists who spend time at their workbench and are, therefore, in a position to make observations and to take advantage of their luck.

Previous experience may also make observation more rather than less difficult. For example, we believe things to be true when we have seen them ourselves – but it is difficult to guard against optical illusions (Fig. 7.2). This is why scientists, to achieve precision, make careful measurements.

Preconceived ideas. Our ability to see things, or to believe what we see, is restricted by our preconceived ideas. People are reluctant to accept new ideas, especially if these conflict with their beliefs.

When, in 1514, Nicholas Copernicus made observations which indicated that the sun, not Earth, was at the centre of the universe, he was at first reluctant to publish his findings. Religious leaders taught that the world had been created at the centre of the heavens: they insisted that the world was flat, and, in 1616 a congregation of political and religious leaders condemned his work (which had eventually been published in 1543) and placed it on a list of prohibited books.

We also find it difficult to make or to accept observations that are outside our previous experience. It is easy to understand why there was a general mistrust of travellers' tales, before the use of photography and television allowed many people to see things for themselves.

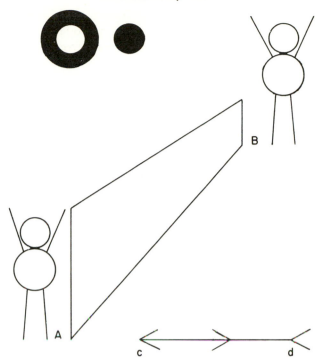

Fig. 7.2 Can you believe what you see? Would the black disc fit into the black ring? Who is the taller, A or B? Where is the mid-point on the horizontal line cd?

Even with these aids to accurate reporting we may still detect bias in accounts of a recent event – reported, for example, by two journalists with opposing political views. If, therefore, it is not possible to know what happened yesterday in London or New York, at an event that was widely reported, it is even more difficult to find out what happened in the past. Indeed, there are countries where it is the duty of historians to abolish the past.

> Such a role is nothing new for historians. In most societies, in most eras, they have received official countenance only on condition that they subscribed to and reinforced the reigning dogmas.

> *The Lessons of History*, Michael Howard (1981)
> Inaugural lecture at University of Oxford.

MAKING AND RECORDING OBSERVATIONS

Before making observations, as part of an investigation, make adequate preparations, then concentrate throughout the observation and be aware of the kinds of difficulties that stand in the way of complete and accurate observation and recording data.

In preparing for an investigation the observer usually plans to record certain kinds of data, perhaps at regular intervals, in a table or *data sheet*, which:

1. Serves as a reminder of when observations are to be made and of what is to be recorded.
2. Facilitates the preparation of records as observations are made, and therefore . . .
3. Helps to ensure that there is a complete and accurate record.

On a data sheet a separate line should be used each time observations are made and there should be a separate column for each measurement that is to be recorded (with a heading indicating what is to be measured and the units of measurement).

The completed data sheet provides a concise record of the observations. Most data sheets include a column for comments so that, for example, any unexpected observations can be recorded and any necessary explanations. If your data sheet is to be included in a report (e.g. for assessment), a carbon copy should be kept (for safe-keeping) as your observations are recorded. Data recorded during observations should not be rewritten because mistakes may be made in copying.

RESULTS OF THE ANALYSIS OF DATA

Observations may be tabulated (as they are made) and, once recorded, are called data. The word *data* refers to facts of any kind: things known to be true. It is incorrect, therefore, to refer to real data or raw data.

Data recorded, in order as observations are made, may not be easy to interpret. The next step in an investigation, therefore, is usually their analysis. With numerical data this analysis may involve the use of statistical methods. However, calculations may not be needed. It may be sufficient to present the data in a diagram.

If data can be interpreted without analysis we may say that the result of the investigation is obvious. If statistical analysis is necessary, the result of this analysis is called a *result*. It is easy, therefore, to distinguish between data and results, although some people use these words incorrectly — as if they were synonyms.

Note particularly that no amount of care in the rearrangement or statistical analysis of data can compensate for inadequate preparation, for lack of care in observation, or for errors in measuring or recording. Careful observation and precise measurement come first, accompanied by the preparation of accurate records. Statistical analysis may then be desirable, but the results should be interpreted with care. For example, always remember the following points.

1. The result should not be expressed in more places of decimals than are present in the least accurately known component of the calculation; otherwise your result will appear to be more accurate than is possible with the method of measurement used in obtaining the data.
2. If things are improbable this does not mean that they never happen, and they may happen in your investigation.
3. If two things are correlated this does not mean that one is necessarily the cause of the other.
4. If a curved or straight line can be drawn through the data points on a graph, this does not mean that they should be so connected. To do so is to infer and imply that intermediate points (had you recorded them) would have been on this line.

PREPARING A REPORT ON AN INVESTIGATION

If you are expected to write an account of an investigation, or of any practical exercise, you should be given sufficient information and advice about what is expected in your particular course (for example, see p. 131).

In practical classes stay until the end. Make full use of these opportunities to learn by handling materials, practising techniques, making observations, and asking questions. Try to complete practical exercises and prepare neat records (date, title, materials, methods and observations) in class, so that you need spend little more time on them. The practice of copying out notes neatly at home is unacceptable because, almost inevitably, mistakes are made (see p. 76).

Instead of spending time on *writing up* practical work, more time should be devoted to thinking about the purpose of the exercise (which should be stated clearly in your *Introduction*) and considering what can be learned from it (in your *Discussion* and *Conclusions*).

8

Read and learn

There are many things that you could not find out for yourself, by observation, even in a lifetime. You must therefore make time for reading books and other publications as sources of information and ideas. Reading is a key to knowledge: a good library is a university that is open to everyone. Indeed, undergraduate students attend lectures and other organized classes but are still said to be *reading* for a degree.

So many books and journals are published every year that it is impossible for any library to buy them all. However, this does not mean that every year there is more for students to learn. On the contrary, observing things that are not understood may be followed by the formulation of hypotheses. Further observations may provide evidence that helps people to reject some hypotheses, so that more knowledge means that there may be less for students to learn. Also, after many observations have been made, links are seen between previously isolated facts and things seem to fall into place. Recognizing a pattern makes things easier to understand.

Some Greek philosophers attempted to record all knowledge. No one could think of doing this today: so much is known. As a result people specialize; it is said that we learn more and more about less and less. In most degree courses the student starts by studying a variety of subjects but specializes, in later years, in aspects of one subject. Syllabuses, therefore, do not cover the whole of any subject. Only selected aspects are introduced in lectures, tutorials, practical classes etc.

DECIDE WHAT TO READ

In most subjects you will not be expected to read the whole of every article or book mentioned in lectures or included in the reading lists provided at the start of a course. Other students will tell you which books they found interesting and useful, but remember that their needs and their evaluation may differ from yours. You need to develop the ability to test and assess any composition for yourself – carefully but *in no more time than is necessary*.

Preliminary survey

To test a book, undertake a quick survey or trial reading, but *read no further than you consider necessary*. Certain questions will be in your mind:

What do I want to know?
Is this book likely to be useful to me?
If it is, should I refer to certain pages, read selected chapters, read the whole book, or just note the full bibliographic details (see p. 175) for future reference?

Look not only at the title but also to see if there is a subtitle: this is printed on the title page, immediately below the title, but not necessarily on the cover. The title and subtitle, together, should give a good indication of what the book is about.

Is this publication sufficiently up-to-date for your present needs? Glance at the date on the reverse of the title page, to see when the book was published and how recently it was revised, so that you will know how up-to-date the information given in the book could be. Note that a book is normally revised for a new edition but not for a reprint.

Is it at the right level for you at this stage in your course? Read the preface which should indicate the author's purpose and intentions. This may tell you that the book is an introduction to the subject, or that it is for advanced students, or that it is a textbook for a particular course.

What is its scope? Scan the table of contents. This also indicates the author's approach, not only by the selection of material for inclusion but also by the order of chapters. From the sequence of topics and the scope of the book, you can see how the author is trying to achieve his purpose. You can see if the book as a whole is likely to provide a balanced treatment of the subject or is concerned mainly with selected aspects.

Does it contain the information you require? Use the contents page or the index so that you can look up something you are already familiar with, to see how the topic is treated in this book. Look up topics in which you are currently interested and read the relevant paragraphs.

How do these parts fit into the composition as a whole? Skim through the book. Read a paragraph or two in each chapter and the headings, and the chapter summaries if there are any. Look at the diagrams and tables. Read especially the last few pages.

Is this book likely to be useful to you? Look at other books before deciding which are likely to be of most use to you. This is particularly important when buying a textbook for your course. However, when selecting books in a library, always consider if each book is relevant to your immediate needs. You may need a general introduction to the subject or a book on a particular aspect. Perhaps you need both so that you can read one chapter from the introduction and selected pages from the other. If a book looks useful, always consider how you should use it.

DECIDE HOW TO READ

If you read and re-read in an attempt to fix things in your mind, your reading is likely to become more and more passive. In re-reading you recognize what you have seen before, rather than learning, and your mind may even be on other things.

As a student *your reading must be active.* In reading, as in other aspects of study, take control of your reading. *Decide* whether to read, which parts to read, and how to read. Just as in driving a car you can brake by going into a lower gear, so in reading you can spend more time on a passage than is worthwhile by employing a reading technique that is not suited to your immediate purpose.

There is more than one way to read a book: you do not have to start on page one and read through to the end. Read according to *your purpose*. Read some books to enjoy the language and the story. Use others as sources of information and ideas. Usually, as a student, you will be: surveying the contents pages of textbooks to discover the scope of the subject, to identify its parts, and to see the approaches of different authors; or reading before classes so that you can benefit more from class work than would otherwise be possible; or looking for information on specific points; or undertaking background reading to confirm and extend your knowledge.

Scanning

Scan the contents pages or index, so that you can go directly to relevant pages of a book, encyclopaedia or journal. If you cannot find a word in the index, try a synonym. Then, if necessary, look at the contents pages to see which chapter or section is most likely to contain the information you require. Scan these pages – not reading them but *looking for particular words* – so that you find relevant sentences quickly. Read these carefully.

Skim reading

When you find a book that contains the information you require, let your eyes skim the pages. You do not need to read every word. Notice the signposts provided by the author: chapter headings, subheadings, words in **bold print** or *italics*, and numbered lists. Look at the tables and diagrams. Read the first paragraph of each chapter, and perhaps the first sentence of each paragraph – which will probably indicate what the chapter or paragraph is about. Read the chapter summaries. In this skim reading you will ignore some paragraphs and even some chapters because they seem irrelevant to your present needs. In this way you will find relevant parts quickly, select relevant material that is new to you, and see how this fits into an organized whole. It will help you, to get a quick overview, if you do not wish to spend long on reading a composition, to *read for the main idea* instead of reading every word.

Rapid reading

When children learn to read the letters are unfamiliar and it is necessary, at first, to say each letter aloud before pronouncing the word as a whole. As the words become familiar they start to read word by word, without difficulty, but may still read aloud. Many adults read slowly because they have not got beyond this word by word stage. The eyes focus on each word and, perhaps, each word is mouthed even though it is not spoken. Saying or mouthing words prevents faster reading – because most people can learn to read much faster than they can speak.

Slow reading is unlikely to be a handicap in studying most subjects, but if you have to do a lot of reading you may wish to increase your reading speed. Check that you do not mouth the words, or stare at each word as you come to it. If necessary, make an effort to improve your vocabulary by reading good prose and looking up unfamiliar words in a dictionary, so that you are not held up by words that you do not understand.

To increase your reading speed, even if you already read quite quickly, make your eyes move forward, allowing them to stop only four, three or two times, as you learn to move them faster along each line. You will soon find that you are reading two or three words at a time. Do not allow your eyes, as they move forward, to glance back at words gone by. Practice rapid reading regularly – at first with light reading matter.

Reading faster does not mean reading non-stop. *Adjust your method of reading and your reading speed according to your purpose* (see Table 8.1). When necessary, pause for thought, consider what you have read in relation to your previous knowledge, and make notes so that your reading is active. Reading faster will not mean that you assimilate less. On the contrary, you are likely to concentrate more easily, grasp the author's meaning sooner, understand better, and remember more.

Read critically

Whatever you read, be it a whole book or one chapter, or a short article, always begin with a preliminary survey. Note the author's approach, purpose, and style of writing. *Consider your purpose.* Why are you spending time on this activity?

Table 8.1 Reading to some purpose: adjust your method of reading and your reading speed according to your purpose

Technique	Purpose
Trial reading	Quick survey so that you can decide if, when and how the composition may be of use to you.
Scanning	Rapid search for particular words, for example in the index or on text pages.
Skimming	Quick overview of a composition to find parts that are of immediate interest, and to see how these fit in as part of the composition.
Rapid reading	Light reading for pleasure, and as part of active study.
Critical reading	Slower reading, to weigh and consider, to assess, and perhaps to make notes.

Do you have to answer a question that calls for description, criticism, evaluation etc. (see p. 121)? If you are looking for information (details relating to topics) you will scan to find the relevant page or pages quickly. If you are looking for ideas (additional topics) you may skim read to find them quickly. In either case, having selected the parts that are worth active study, you will understand, learn and remember more if you read them twice. First read quickly, as in reading a novel, and then undertake a more critical reading.

Concentrate.
Think carefully to make sure that you understand.
Look back, if necessary, to check the stages in an argument.
Be prepared to consider opinions that differ from your own.
Weigh the evidence and look for contradictions.
Read with an enquiring and critical mind.

If the author asks a question, consider your answer before you read on. Ask yourself questions. Why is this relevant? What does this mean? Is the evidence convincing? Is the composition biased? What have I learned? Such questions will help you to concentrate and to think critically. For example, see p. 108, *Criticize the work of other writers.*

Your reactions, as you read, should be influenced by your previous experience just as an author, in writing, builds upon his experiences. You should not believe every word that you read. Try to distinguish evidence from opinion. Remember that even when there is a basis of fact in every paragraph, the interpretation may be wrong.

Many things are written to convince or to persuade: they are not impartial. You must weigh the evidence presented and try to make up your own mind. Read critically and consider how the information and ideas presented contribute to your understanding and fit in with your knowledge gained from other sources. You may conclude, having considered different sides of an argument, that the truth is not known.

At school you may have thought that every word in your textbooks was to be believed and remembered. However, the more you read books by specialists the more you will find that there are many points on which they disagree. This is why it is best to use more than one textbook on each aspect of your course and to consult other sources of information and ideas. As a student you should not be trying to learn what you have been told or what you have read: by thinking and questioning you should be aiming at a better understanding, as you master your subject.

MAKE NOTES AS YOU READ

Many of the books you consult are not your own. You should not mark them in any way. Furthermore, you are advised not to mark even your own textbooks. When you first read a book you will be learning about the subject and, especially in your first year at college, you may not know enough or have the experience to decide what is worth marking. Also, if you look at a book for one purpose you could mark things that will not be relevant when you next consult the book – for another purpose. Your earlier marks may then distract and mislead you. It is better to make concise additions to your lecture notes (including relevant page numbers from your textbooks) so that if necessary you can find the same paragraphs quickly if you need them again.

Make notes on wide-lined A4 paper, as used for your lecture notes (see p. 57). First record complete bibliographic details of any publication from which you extract ideas or information (see Fig. 8.1). You will need these details if you wish to refer to the same publication again, or include them in a bibliography or list of references (see p. 134).

Authors may present information in writing, in tables, or in

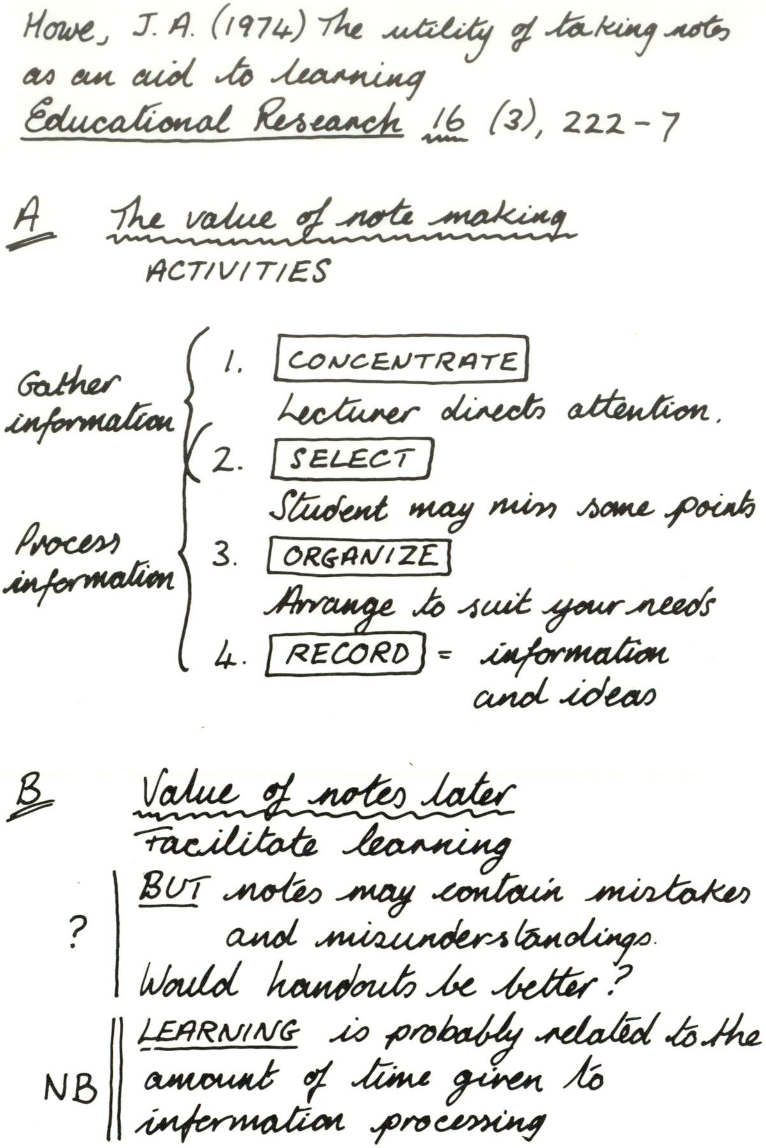

Howe, J. A. (1974) The utility of taking notes
as an aid to learning
<u>Educational Research</u> 16 (3), 222 - 7

<u>A</u>   <u>The value of note making</u>
              ACTIVITIES

Gather   1. | CONCENTRATE |
information   Lecturer directs attention.

              2. | SELECT |
                  Student may miss some points

Process   3. | ORGANIZE |
information   Arrange to suit your needs

              4. | RECORD | = information
                                and ideas

<u>B</u>   <u>Value of notes later</u>
          Facilitate learning
     ?   <u>BUT</u> notes may contain mistakes
                and misunderstandings.
          Would handouts be better?
          <u>LEARNING</u> is probably related to the
     NB   amount of time given to
          information processing

Fig. 8.1   Notes on an article by Howe, J. A., published in a research journal.

diagrams, but information presented in one way will not usually be repeated in another. You must therefore study the tables and illustrations as well as the text.

From some pages of a book you may think it worthwhile to make detailed notes, *in your own words,* and to include simple diagrams and flow-charts. However, make sure that your notes on the whole book are concise. Writing out or photocopying long passages, or making detailed notes, may fill your subject files with useless clutter, and so is likely to be a waste of your time. It is better and usually quicker to prepare concise notes and to record page numbers so that you can read important passages from your textbooks several times. In other words, try to store information in your brain rather than on paper. Also remember that your notes are for using, not for storing, and if they are too long they will be of little use either in your studies or in your final revision prior to an examination.

Do not make notes as you read for the first time. Start by reading quickly so that you can follow the author's explanations and arguments, see connections, and find the parts which are worth close attention. Then read these parts again, select carefully, and make concise notes (see Fig. 8.1). By recording a key word, phrase or sentence about each paragraph, you can reconstruct the author's topic outline (c.f. Fig. 8.1 with Fig. 8.2).

If you add your own comments or evaluations, mark them by a vertical line and your initials in the margin. Mark anything that is undecided, or that you question or do not understand, by a vertical line in the margin and a question mark. Make a note, especially, of the answers to your questions or of anything new to you. Later, to clear up any difficulties, use the index or look at other books, or try to find out for yourself, or ask someone who knows, until (if possible) you find the answers to your questions (see p. 51).

At the end of each section or chapter, as you read and make notes, stop to *review your progress* (as you would after a lecture, see p. 52). Skim through the pages again. Relate the parts to the whole. Check that your notes are accurate and that you have recognized the main points. Add your comments and your evaluation. Devoting time to this review will help you to recall much of what you have read, to understand more, to see connections, and to refresh your memory and so fix in your mind those things that you wish to remember.

Then, for *revision,* try to recall and list the author's main points from memory (see Table 8.2). Check to confirm that you have

Table 8.2 How to read*

Stages in active reading	Activities
1. Survey	*Consider your purpose* What is this composition about? Is it sufficiently up-to-date? Does it contain the information you need?
2. Question	*Ask yourself* Should I read it? If so, which parts should I read? How should I read it?
3. Read critically	*Skim read* selected parts. *Read* again. *Select. Organize* to suit your purpose. *Make notes.*
4. Review	*Consider* what you have read. *Check your notes.* Have you extracted the information you need and arranged it to suit your purpose.
5. Revise	*Remember.* *List* main points from memory.

* Note that this is not the only way to read, but use these suggestions to help you to think about why and how you read, and how you may be able to improve your reading techniques.
Always define your purpose, read according to your purpose, and read actively – not passively.

remembered correctly. Just as before reading you should decide what you want to know (see p. 68), so after reading you should check that you have extracted this information.

Making notes is a part of active study which helps you to maintain attention and to think, so that you can select the author's main points, evidence, examples, steps in an argument, and conclusions. In making you think, making notes helps you to understand. Writing is an activity which makes you repeat selected points and so helps you to learn and remember them. You may not remember everything as a result of this first reading, but you can refresh your memory from your notes – without having to read the whole book again. In this way the notes may be useful when you prepare a topic outline (see p. 105) as you plan an answer to a question set in course work.

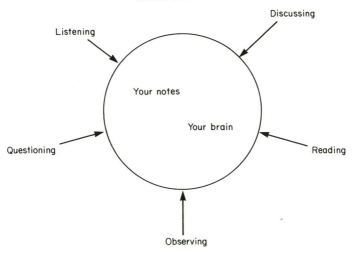

Fig. 8.2 The central place of your notes in active study. Sources of information are indicated by arrows. Your notes should be much more than a store: they should be arranged to facilitate collecting, selecting and organizing relevant material – as an aid to understanding, learning and revising.

One set of notes

Add to or modify your lecture notes in the light of your increased knowledge or better understanding, so that you have only one set of notes on each aspect of your work (see p. 145). You may find it helpful to use black ink for your lecture notes and blue ink for other work so that additions can be distinguished easily.

Your notes become an irreplacable study aid. They provide a framework upon which additional facts and ideas can be hung, so that you can associate this new material with what you already know. This facilitates learning and revision (see Fig. 8.2). The value of your notes increases as your course proceeds. They must, therefore, be kept in a safe place. Do not lend them to anyone; and on journeys keep them with you all the time – do not let them out of your sight. You cannot afford to lose the results of one, two or three years' work.

UNDERSTAND AND SELECT

Comprehension tests

Every question set in course work and examinations is a test of your ability to understand. If you do not understand exactly what is required you may answer the wrong question or give an answer that is incomplete (see p. 156). Furthermore, careful reading and comprehension is the first step in making good notes, and in preparing a précis or summary. Teachers who neglect the teaching of comprehension, précis writing and summarizing skills, should appreciate that pupils or students who cannot do these things well are handicapped in other aspects of their work.

Writing a précis

In reducing the length of a composition you should omit all figurative language or ornament, anything of secondary importance, and all digressions and superfluous words. With practice you will grasp the essentials of a composition at first reading and writing a précis will become easier.

Regular practice in précis writing will help you to learn aspects of effective study: careful reading and comprehension, the exercise of judgement in selecting the essentials, and accurate reporting. Preparing a précis will also help you to learn more about *selected aspects* of your work. For practice, try writing a précis of a leading article from a good newspaper, an article from a magazine or journal, or one of your own essays. Recognizing superfluous words and phrases in other people's work (see p. 109 and p. 119) will help you to be more critical of your own writing and to develop a more economical and direct style.

Writing a summary

A summary of an article, or of a passage from a book, includes only the main points. It is like a topic outline but is written in complete sentences. Most of your own compositions in course work and examinations will be too short to require a summary. Indeed, an essay should come to some conclusion and should not end with the repetition of points already effectively made (see p. 117). However, practice in preparing good summaries (e.g. of recorded talks, see p. 48, and of articles – when you have more time to select) will help you to develop your ability to recognize stages in an argument or topics in a topic outline. It will help you to learn to distinguish quickly between main points and supporting detail (evidence, examples and illustrations).

If you have difficulty in making good notes in lectures, this may be because you try to write too much: you may record too many details yet miss important points. Practice in selecting main points from a composition, when you have more time for thought, will increase your confidence when you have to listen, select, and make notes in lectures.

If you have difficulty in writing essays and reports, perhaps you include too much detail or perhaps you omit essential points. In your own compositions, as in making lecture notes, you need the confidence to recognize main points and to include only the necessary supporting detail. What you consider to be the essentials, and what is necessary detail, will depend upon why you are writing and for whom you are writing.

If you feel that you are not doing as well as you should in examinations, perhaps you know the answers but have difficulty in selecting material for inclusion and organizing an effective answer in the time available. Again your difficulty is partly one of selection. Preparing summaries of other people's compositions and topic outlines for your own, will help you to do better work.

Writing summaries of articles, and of important passages from books, should help you to make useful additions to your notes. In this way, as with précis writing, preparing a summary is a method of active study that makes you concentrate, makes you confirm that you understand, and makes you be selective, and so is an aid to learning and remembering.

Some students have difficulty in remembering because they try to remember too much. Except for things that must be remembered word for word (see p. 62), rote learning is a waste of time. Practice in preparing summaries should help such students to select only key words and phrases so that they have less to learn. Selection is easy, with most compositions, because the first sentence of each paragraph is the topic sentence. Topic sentences and subheadings draw your attention to what the author considers to be the main points. For practice, try writing a summary of an article that includes a summary. Then compare your summary with that prepared by the author.

GET TO KNOW USEFUL REFERENCE BOOKS

Your textbooks may provide all the information you need for a first examination at school, but in more advanced courses and as soon as you begin to think of yourself not as a pupil but as a student, you must learn to make effective use of other books and of other resources available in your college library and in other local libraries. Remember that the librarians are anxious to advise and help if you have any questions about using the library or if you cannot find the information you require (Fig. 8.3).

THE LIBRARIANS ARE ANXIOUS TO HELP

Fig. 8.3   The book number in the catalogue will help you to find a particular book, which has this number marked on its spine.

Dictionaries. In a dictionary you can find the correct spelling, pronunciation, and meaning of words. A good dictionary (see p. 174) will also give the origin of each word and its current uses. In addition to dictionaries of English and of American English, there are dictionaries of the technical terms of your subject, and there are dictionaries of abbreviations. There are many other kinds of dictionaries which you should see in the reference section of any good library.

Encyclopaedias. The best known encyclopaedias in the English language include the *Encyclopaedia Britannica* and *Chambers' Encyclopaedia*. If you require an introduction to any subject, an encyclopaedia is a good starting point. However, it takes a long time to prepare or to revise an encyclopaedia and you will need to look elsewhere if you require up-to-date information.

Directories. Telephone directories are a useful source of names and addresses. Other directories provide similar information about, for example, particular trades or professions.

Handbooks. A handbook, as its name implies, should be a concise reference book. It provides concise information on one subject, for your day-to-day use (see p. 175).

Books. Learn how to find the books on a particular subject or the books by a particular author, in your college library and in the other libraries that you use, so that you can find information quickly. Find out how books are classified in these libraries (see Table 8.3). The book number given in the catalogue will help you to find a particular book – which has this number marked on its spine – on a shelf in an appropriate part of the library.

Journals, magazines and newspapers. Look at the periodicals taken regularly by your library. Current issues are usually on display, perhaps in a separate room.

Periodicals contain original and review articles, which may be of interest to you, but there are many thousands of periodicals and most libraries can subscribe to only a few. You should therefore know that there are abstracting and indexing journals which help people undertaking a literature search to find articles that are likely to be of interest. There are also computer-based information retrieval

Table 8.3 Three systems for classifying books in libraries (from Barrass, R. (1982) *Students Must Write*, Methuen & Co Ltd, London)

The ten classes of the Dewey Decimal System	Universal Decimal System	Library of Congress System
000 General works	0	A
Reference books (030)	03	AE
100 Philosophy	1	B
Psychology (150)	15	BF
200 Religion	2	BL
300 Social sciences	3	H
400 Languages	4	P
500 Pure sciences	5	Q
600 Applied sciences	6	
700 The Arts	7	N
800 Literature	8	P
900 Geography (910)	91	G
Biography (920)	92	CT
History (930)	93	C

services. Once you have complete bibliographic details, a publication can be obtained on inter-library loan.

OTHER SOURCES OF INFORMATION

There may be collections of photographs, maps, recordings, tape-slide sets, video tapes, and films, containing material that would be of interest to you. These may be available in an audio-visual aids section of your library, or they may be kept in map rooms or language laboratories, or other specialist rooms, in appropriate teaching departments. There may also be radio and televisions talks and films, relevant to your studies, that you can receive at home.

Programmed learning

Most books are written for reading or reference, but some provide programmed instruction. You must engage in other activities, including making choices and checking progress. There is an attempt to confirm that you understand one topic before you are allowed to proceed to the next. Work through programmed books, relevant to your studies, to see if you find programmed learning helpful. If you do, use each chapter as a lesson. Do not try to read the whole book at one sitting. Use programmed texts in addition to your standard textbooks, not as a substitute.

Computer assisted learning

In Computer Assisted Learning (CAL) and Computer Assisted Instruction (CAI) each course begins with a title and a list of the things it will help you to learn. CAI gives instruction and then, to test your knowledge and understanding, gives you practice. CAL gives you information, asks you to use this information, and then tests what you have learned.

Features of these courses are as follows:

1. You can progress at your own pace.
2. You can stop at any point and pick up, later, where you left off.
3. Different approaches to the subject may be provided so that you can choose to learn topics in an order that suits you best (e.g. by following on directly from what you already know about the subject).
4. All the instruction is presented on a screen (see Fig. 8.4).

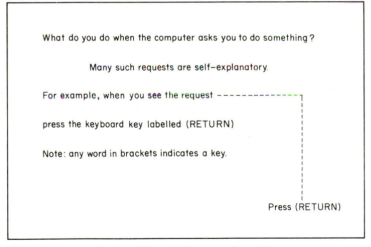

Fig. 8.4   Computer Assisted Instruction: words on the screen at one step in a course. Individual programmes differ slightly in arrangement.

Table 8.4 One question from a multiple choice test, as part of a computer assisted learning programme

Computer	Indicate the word which comes closest in meaning to 'Feierabend' in the following sentence.
	Beamte haben einen mehr freizeitbetonten als arbeitsbezogenen Feierabend.
	Type A, B or C: A Freizeit B Zeit nach Arbeitsschluss C Party
Learner	A
Computer	'Freizeit' means 'leisure' or 'free time'. You are looking for an expression with the sense of 'free time after finishing work'.
Learner	B
Computer	That is better. 'Feierabend' has the sense 'free time after finishing work'.

Note 1. The computer can be programmed to guide the learner towards the right answer following a mistake.
2. Table based on Davies, G. (1982) *Computers, Language and Language Learning*, Centre for Information on Language Teaching and Research, London.

5. In contrast with traditional learning methods, in which a pen and paper are used, it is usually necessary to type your answers on a keyboard.
6. Your answers appear on the screen.
7. If you make a mistake, you may be able to delete your answer by pressing a key.
8. When you are satisfied with your answer you can press the key which, according to an instruction on the screen, takes you on to the next step if your answer is correct.
9. If your answer is incorrectly entered, your attention is drawn to the mistake. You can then delete letters and make corrections.

To summarize, the computer provides the instruction and information, asks questions, evaluates your answers and provides immediate feedback, taking you through the course step by step. This is an active form of learning, because you are made to think (by being given not only information to consider but also questions to answer) and if you do not remember something you can work through part or the whole of the course again.

These programmes, like books, vary in quality. To write a good one, the author must know the subject, know how to teach the subject, and know how to programme effectively. Do not be put off, therefore, if you do not like the first programmes you try.

Except for mathematics questions, in which the computer can check the answer by calculation, the answers to questions set in the programme have to be stored in a file. The computer will then accept only this stored answer as correct. If you type in a different but correct answer (e.g. expressing the correct answer in different words) the computer will not recognize it as being correct. To avoid this problem, a question may be presented at the same time as a number of possible answers – a multiple choice test (see Table 8.4). A correct answer may then simply be recognized, and you may think you know something that is not yet fixed in your mind. Alternatively, each question may require a yes/no or true/false answer.

As with programmed texts (p. 95), use computer assisted instruction to complement your standard textbooks, not as a substitute.

9

Write and learn

In discussions, you learn from others and can test your own ideas, but may lose your train of thought or may not have the opportunity to say all that you would have liked to say. In contrast, in private study you can observe, read, contemplate, and then express the results of your thinking. Without interruption or distraction you can write, correct, revise and if necessary rewrite – until satisfied that this is your best work.

Writing will help you, as a student, to make and record observations, to remember things, to capture thoughts and arrange them in order, and to express your knowledge. It is therefore part of active study. Also, in writing you express yourself. This is why teachers and examiners judge, by your writing in homework and examinations, your knowledge, your understanding, and your ability to organize and communicate thoughts.

In view of the importance of writing in course work and examinations, in applications for employment, and in most professions, consider whether or not your writing could and should be improved. In your writing do you display an educated and lively mind? Does your writing have any of the defects that would cause you to condemn the writing of others (see p. 110 and p. 118)? Does your writing have any of the faults that are commonly encountered by teachers and examiners when they mark students' written work?

FAULTS COMMONLY ENCOUNTERED IN STUDENTS' WRITTEN WORK

Because writing is an expression of thought, the faults considered here indicate lack of thought, insufficient thought, or an inability to think clearly.

(a) Lack of knowledge of the subject

The most common reason for poor performance is a failure to display sufficient knowledge of the subject. This may be because the student does not know the whole answer to the question asked, or it may be due to an inability to communicate the information required in an effective answer.

In course work, when there is an opportunity to seek further information and so to fill gaps, the regular submission of incomplete answers may be due to lack of ability, to lack of thought and effort, or to lack of organization and the consequent ineffective use of time.

(b) Lack of understanding

Many students make the mistake of thinking that information is all that is required. Usually the facts of the matter, by themselves, are not enough.

Include enough detail and enough explanation, to show your knowledge and understanding. Define essential terms (especially those used in the question). Summarize evidence and give an example if it will help to make your point. Show your understanding by including only relevant material and by ensuring that your answer is complete and in good order.

Include simple diagrams (see Figs 7.2 and 9.1) if these will contribute to your explanation, help your reader to understand your answer, and help you to give a more complete answer. Place each diagram as near as you can to the part of the answer to which it applies, but number all diagrams and refer to them in your answer (more than once if necessary). Give each diagram a concise heading or legend and use labelling to draw attention to things that are especially relevant to your answer, but do not waste time on shading.

Do not leave things out of your answer because you think they are too elementary. It is best to mention things if they are relevant, even if

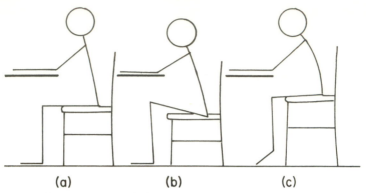

Fig. 9.1 If appropriate, include simple diagrams in your compositions. For example: (a) sitting comfortably; (b) and (c) sitting uncomfortably.

only in passing. Each question is an opportunity to display your knowledge. The reader cannot guess what you know and you can score marks only for what you write.

(c) Lack of evidence

Statements made in any composition should be supported by sufficient evidence and by appropriate examples. Unsupported statements are unconvincing because they are not easily distinguished from opinions. Also, it is usually necessary for a student to demonstrate knowledge of the evidence for – and against – any statement that might be considered controversial.

Authorities are not necessarily correct (see p. 74) and authority is no substitute for evidence, but the sources of any ideas that are not your own, especially if these are new or controversial, should be stated (see p. 119). Quoting sources also helps you to indicate that you have done some background reading and are taking more than a beginner's interest in your work.

It is also useful in course work, for your own future reference as well as for the reader, to include a bibliography (of sources consulted) or a list of references (of sources cited in the composition) at the end of every composition (see p. 134).

(d) Lack of logic

Arguments developed within a paragraph, or in successive paragraphs, should lead to a logical conclusion. Logical thought, starting from true premises, leads to a valid conclusion. But thinking illogically, even from true premises, could lead to a valid conclusion only by accident.

(e) Bias

People are inclined to ignore or reject evidence that is contrary to their own preconceived ideas, or evidence that is contrary to what is believed to be currently accepted public opinion (see p. 75). However, scholarly writing should be free from bias.

Speculation, if it is necessary, should be clearly indicated by such words as *may*, *possibly* and *perhaps*. And things first mentioned as possibilities should not later be stated as if they were facts. Nor is it acceptable to go beyond the available evidence: extrapolation is not a reliable method for reaching conclusions. Remember, also, that if two things are correlated it should not be assumed that one is necessarily the cause of the other (see p. 77).

In advertising and politics, for example, it is usual to use emotive language, instead of evidence, and to exaggerate and present only the advantages of a product or selected facts that are in accordance with party dogma. But scholars, seeking the truth, should avoid emotive language and should present evidence for and evidence against — unless they are asked to do otherwise. Where appropriate they should present a variety of opinions, to show that they are aware of different interpretations even if they conclude by supporting one point of view.

(f) Lack of relevance of the whole or part of an answer

Including irrelevant material may be the result of misunderstanding the question, or of a failure to consider exactly what is required (see p. 64, pp. 121–4), or from digression. Whatever the cause, it is always a waste of time. No marks can be scored for information that is not required. If, therefore, you include anything in your answer that is not obviously relevant, you must make clear why you consider it to be relevant.

Lack of relevance is inevitable if the wrong question is answered. This may happen in course work because the question has been copied incorrectly from a blackboard or from a friend's notes. It may also happen in examinations if a candidate prepares an answer during revision and then is asked a slightly different question (see p. 156).

It is a good idea in course work, but a waste of time in examinations, to write the question (the exact words and punctuation marks), when the question is set, at the top of a clean sheet of paper. This same paper can then be used for the first sheet of your answer.

(g) Repetition

Some students write answers which follow closely a lecture on the subject. This is likely to result not only in the inclusion of material that is irrelevant in an answer to a particular question but also in repetition. The techniques of the lecturer are not appropriate for the writer. Unless it is recorded, a lecture can be heard once only. The lecturer may therefore repeat important points for emphasis. For example, the lecture may begin with a statement of the topics to be considered. These will then be considered one at a time in a logical order. The important points may finally be included in a brief summary. In writing, however, each main point should normally be made not three times but just once because, if necessary, the words can be read more than once.

(h) Lack of originality

Your answer to a question should be the result of your own thought. An original presentation is not achieved by simply reproducing notes made in a lecture; this course of action is likely to result in an answer that is similar to that of many other students who are taking the same course. Nor is originality achieved by copying appropriate passages from books: apart from other considerations these will be written in different styles and, obviously, none will be your own.

Copying other people's work, if it is the work of a fellow student, is cheating. And taking extracts from books or other published work, and then presenting the words as your own – without acknowledging their source – is plagiarism (stealing thoughts). Neither cheating nor plagiarism is acceptable in scholarly writing.

To benefit from lectures, from tutorials and other discussions, from your own observations, and from your background reading (see Fig. 6.4, p. 69) always think before you consult your notes (see Fig. 9.3). Select information that is relevant and answer the questions asked; arrange the material in your own way and *present the results of your own thought*.

Indicate extracts by indentation and by giving their source (as on p. 72). Indicate the source of ideas or information presented, especially if the views expressed are new or controversial, by either a number or a name and date in the text (as explained on p. 134), immediately after your summary of this author's observations, conclusions, or views, and by giving complete bibliographic details at the end of your composition. However, in examinations it is enough to include the name of the author and either the date of the publication or its title (or both, see p. 17) in your composition.

An original presentation does not necessarily include original material. As a result of independent thought you may combine ideas and information in new ways to produce new associations and new insights. This is creativity (see also p. 105).

(i) Lack of balance

An unbalanced answer, in which some parts of a question receive too much attention and other parts receive too little, is the result of lack of planning and, in an examination, perhaps also to an inefficient allocation of time (see also Fig. 9.2).

BALANCE IS IMPORTANT IN WRITING - AS IN MOST THINGS

Fig. 9.2 Carry at least a few sheets of paper and a pen so that you can record interesting observations, bright ideas, or notes of things to do, as they come to mind.

(j) Lack of order – wholeness – unity

When the paragraphs are not in a logical order this is another sign that the writer did not work to a plan. Words such as therefore, moreover, and however, help the writer to make connections. But without planning such connections cannot be properly made, logical argument is difficult, and an easy flow of ideas is impossible.

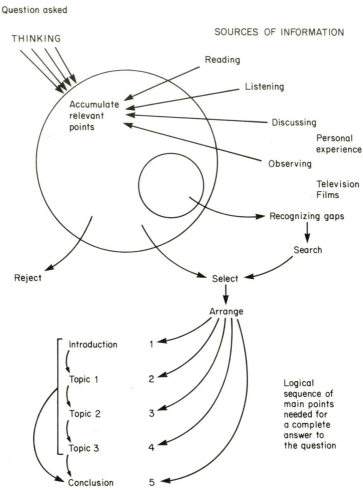

Fig. 9.3   Thinking about a question and planning your answer.

WRITE ANSWERS TO QUESTIONS

Creativity

The first stages in composition (thinking and planning) are active study techniques (see p. 64).

Before writing you must decide what you wish to say and how best to say it. Listing ideas and preparing a plan (a topic outline) may take a few minutes or several weeks, according to the amount of time that is available or necessary.

In course work start thinking about the question soon after it is set (see p. 64). Prepare some notes and a plan for your answer (see p. 66) at least a week before you start to write (see Table 4.5, p. 33). This will give you time to look for any additional information you require, and to do any necessary background reading. In living with your ideas, you will also have time for second thoughts. By looking for a different approach and a different arrangement of your material, you can make yourself think again and give yourself a basis for choice. As a result you may keep to your first plan, or modify it, or perhaps prefer a new one. You will find that your first thoughts are not always the best. Indeed, most people can benefit by putting their plan on one side for a time and then thinking afresh.

Thinking and making notes – capturing your thoughts before starting to write – is a creative process (Fig. 9.3). You use your imagination and your judgement in deciding what to include, how to begin, how to preserve order and make connections, and how to end. As a result of your thought, you put things together in a new way – you make new associations, gain new insights, and achieve a deeper understanding.

As a student you must learn in three ways:

1. By reading or by being told.
2. By finding out for yourself (by observation).
3. By thinking (considering what you know and making new associations).

As you think about your subject things may seem to fall into place. You then achieve a deeper understanding.

In science discoveries are made not only by seeing things for the first time but also, for example, by naming the things observed, and by arranging them in new ways. Observation, naming things, and arranging them, may result in the recognition of order — as in the systems for naming and classifying living organisms devised by Linnaeus in the 18th century, and in the periodic classification of chemical elements proposed by Mendeleyev in the 19th century.

Good ideas come to mind not only when you are working at a task but also when you are relaxing or thinking of other things. Order may then be recognized where previously things seemed only confusing. And the simplicity of this orderly arrangement may be a source of pleasure — as in the simplicity of an efficient engineering construction or a concise mathematical proof.

Most professional writers carry at least a few sheets of paper and a pen so that they can record interesting observations, bright ideas, or notes of things to do, as they come to mind. You are advised to do the same so that you can note, for example, a suitable introduction for a composition you are planning, or an additional topic, or a revised order of paragraphs, or thoughts arising during conversation with lecturers or fellow students. Unless you capture any thoughts that you wish to remember, by making a note, you may find that you cannot recollect them later. It is best to make notes, and to incorporate these at appropriate places in your lecture notes, or in your notes for a composition, at the next opportunity (see p. 89).

Making a note is an aid not only to remembering but also to creativity. And with a pencil and paper in your pocket you are ready to write anywhere and at any time. This is one way in which you can make effective use of a few minutes spent waiting for an appointment or half an hour on a bus or train.

Write at one sitting

It is best to write your answer at one sitting. In examinations you have to do this; and in all written work it is best to get into the habit of writing quickly to ensure continuity which makes for easy reading.

If you have mastered your subject you will be selective. This, and the need to complete the composition within a word limit (in homework or course work) or a time limit (in examinations especially), should help you to avoid verbosity (see p. 120).

Descriptive and imaginative writing, and flowery language, which are encouraged at school for some English essays, are not appropriate in answering most questions, especially in other subjects. Your purpose will usually be to explain something – to convey information and ideas. Your writing should not usually be subjective (based on the imagination) but should be objective (based on evidence and supported by examples). Your writing should have the following characteristics: accuracy, clarity, completeness, conciseness, orderliness, and simplicity. In conveying information and advice, arrange your thoughts in an effective order and then try to *express yourself as clearly and simply as you can.*

Write on wide-lined A4 paper (see p. 57) and leave wide margins and space at the bottom of each sheet (especially the last) for the marker's comments and corrections.

Use your topic outline as a guide

Preparing an outline helps to put you in the right frame of mind for writing, and if your outline is a good one it will probably be similar to the marking scheme that will be used in assessing your work.

Most of the faults considered earlier in this chapter are the results of a lack of planning. By following a topic outline you can:

1. Begin well.
2. Concentrate on one topic at a time.
3. Write quickly.
4. Keep to the point (ensure relevance).
5. Emphasise your main points (topics).
6. Deal with each topic fully in one place.
7. Keep moving at a proper pace, to hold your reader's attention.
8. Avoid repetition.
9. Maintain order.
10. Number tables and diagrams and put each one in the most appropriate place.
11. Make proper connections so that your reader can follow your train of thought.
12. Maintain control.
13. Ensure completeness and coherence – wholeness – unity.
14. Arrive at an effective conclusion.

With your topic outline complete, look again at the question to confirm that your plan does provide the basis for a good answer.

1. Check that you have understood exactly what is required (see

Tables 10.2 and 10.3, pp. 123–4). Try to make your topic outline identical with the examiner's marking scheme.

2. Consider how your answer will be assessed. For example, if you are studying for a degree, see Table 9.1.

CRITICIZE THE WORK OF OTHER WRITERS

You can learn to criticize your own compositions, and then improve them, by first looking critically at the work of others. For example, consider the following extracts.

> It generally takes longer to say something than to read it. It has been estimated for example that the main news bulletin contains less words than a page of *The Times*. Broadcasts therefore have to be even more selective than newspapers. In the case of television, pictures as well as words have to be selected.
>
> Television news . . . is supposed not to have an editorial stance; . . . to be objective and uncommitted – to be balanced. However, this is in itself a particular stance, which is all the more powerful because of its air of disinterested authority. How far news programmes can be uncommitted is a matter of argument. Lord Reith, the first Director General of the BBC, once said that the BBC could never be neutral between right and wrong – and everyone's ideas of what is right and wrong differ to some degree.
>
> Just as newspapers have journalists and editors, so broadcasting has scriptwriters, producers and programme planners. What is shown, what it sounds like, depends on their decisions.
>
> *Preparing to Study*, Open University (1979)

Thoughts of a critical reader

Paragraph 1 Comments

1. Is *generally* the right word? Would *usually* be better?
   Is *less* the right word? Would *fewer* be better?
2. Does the main radio news bulletin last for 10 minutes or 30 minutes?
   How long does it take to read every word on a page of *The Times*?
   Does the second sentence provide evidence or an example illus-

trating the point made in the first sentence? If not, does this mean that the first sentence is incorrect?

3. Strictly it is not the broadcast or the newspaper that is selective but the script-writer or editor.

4. Would it be better, instead of the verbose phrase *In the case of television* to write *For television*? Is it always better, instead of using the words *in the case of* to say what you mean?
   Paragraphs 2 and 3   Points for discussion.

5. Because people differ in their opinions about what is right or wrong, can any script-writer or producer be disinterested?

6. Because script-writers and editors have to be selective, only some facts relating to an occurrence can be passed on to the readers. How do you think they decide what to tell you? Should they tell you only the things they expect you to want to know?

See how others write

Study leading articles in good newspapers, and articles in magazines that are relevant to your course of study. Ask yourself these questions.

Does the title capture my interest?
Does the first sentence make me want to read further?
Is each paragraph relevant? Pick out the topic sentence of each paragraph and reconstruct the author's topic outline.
Are the paragraphs in a logical and effective order?
Do they lead to an effective conclusion?
Are the arguments convincing?
Are all your questions answered?

When you have reconstructed the author's topic outline, for any short article that is of interest to you, put the article on one side and then write an article yourself, based on this topic outline. Then compare the two compositions. In this way you will learn more about your subject and you will practise writing. Is your composition as interesting and as easy to read as the original? Repeating this exercise with different short articles, or with extracts from books, will help you to develop your ability to pick out key points, to consider how others organize and present their material, and to develop your own style of writing.

Table 9.1 Scoring marks for a written answer in a degree course

Standard of work	Mark out of 10	Grade
Outstanding *Presentation.* Work neat, well organized and clearly expressed. *Length* appropriate. *Content.* Displaying knowledge and understanding of all aspects of a complete and correct answer to the question asked. Probably including information and ideas gained by reading beyond standard texts, knowledge of recent work, and, for the highest marks, original ideas.	8+	A
Good Displaying knowledge of most or all aspects of a complete answer, but understanding not always made clear, and perhaps giving no indication of background reading. Perhaps longer than is necessary and including some irrelevant material.	6+	B
Average *Answer incomplete:* does not include all essentials. Unnecessary repetition and *poor organization* may indicate an incomplete grasp of the subject, or an inability to communicate effectively. May include *irrelevant material,* indicating that the question was not properly understood.	5	C
Just acceptable	4	D
Answer inaccurate or incomplete: Not up to the required standard.	3	F
Displaying little knowledge and no understanding.	2	F
Displaying no knowledge or including only irrelevant material.	0	F

CHECK YOUR OWN WORK

Remember the four stages in composition: *think*, *plan*, *write* and then *check* your work (see Table 4.5, p. 33).

In examinations check your answer immediately, as you complete it, and then check all your answers again at the end of the examination to ensure that there are no major omissions and to correct obvious mistakes.

In course work put your composition on one side for a few days and then check all the following aspects of your work.

1. Does your answer read easily and does it sound well when read aloud?
2. Have you explained each main point sufficiently? Would an example help the reader?
3. Are your statements supported by sufficient evidence?
4. Is your answer unbiased, and are opinions clearly indicated as such?
5. Have you indicated sources where necessary?
6. Is every sentence relevant and clearly expressed?
7. Is your answer too long? That is to say, is every word, phrase, sentence and paragraph necessary? Have you kept within the word limit stated when the question was set?
8. Have you included any imprecise words such as few, some, several, many, small, and large, which could be replaced by a number? Most readers would prefer to know how many or how large.
9. Is every word legible?
10. Can you find any mistakes? It is better to correct them yourself, if possible, than to lose marks when they are corrected.
11. Are your paragraphs in an effective order? Does each one lead logically to the next? Is your composition as a whole well balanced? Have you paid the right amount of attention to each part of the question? Have you included appropriate sign-posts (headings and letters, see p. 160) to indicate the parts of your answer to the questions set?
12. Is your composition a complete answer to the question set?

You should not get into the habit of writing things more than once. However, if you have spent several weeks preparing and writing a piece of course work, you should be prepared to revise and rewrite your composition if this will improve it – in an attempt to score higher marks.

If you decide to revise your work this does not mean that you are unintelligent. On the contrary, with further thought an intelligent person should be able to improve a first draft. As in editing someone else's work, creativity is involved in checking, criticizing and revising your own compositions. You may recognize irrelevance or illogicality, or decide upon a better arrangement.

HOW COURSE WORK MARKS AFFECT YOUR GRADES

In many colleges both course work marks and examination marks contribute to assessment. That is to say, students are judged not just by their performance over a few days in examinations but also by their effort (or lack of effort) over the whole year – as indicated by the marks scored for homework, practical work etc. However, the assessment of course work presents many problems. For example, it is not possible to know how much help each student has received. Also, plagiarism (see p. 102) may not be detected.

An examination is an attempt to ensure that all students are tested at the same time and under similar conditions. The marks awarded, therefore, are usually considered to provide a more reliable indication than the course-work marks of a student's ability in academic subjects. This is why, in calculating the total mark for each aspect of the work, tested in an examination paper and in related course work, the examination mark usually contributes more than the course work mark to the final mark.

Students should know, from the start of their course, how they will be assessed. If both course work and examination marks contribute to the final mark, they should know how this final mark for each unit is calculated (e.g. 30% course work mark plus 70% examination mark, see Table 9.3).

Students who do not complete assessed course work exercises deprive themselves of practice and of opportunities for learning (see p. 114); and they cannot benefit from the assessors' corrections and suggestions. If course work marks do contribute to the final assessment, the consequences of not handing in course work should be considered. Note, for example, that an obviously capable student (e.g. student C in Table 9.2) may fail in course work, whereas a

Table 9.2 Scoring marks for course work

Student	Marks out of 20 for five course work exercises							Course work	
	1	2	3	4	5		%	Result
A	12	13	9	10	NS	=	44	Pass
B	10	NS	8	6	10	=	34	Fail
C	14	NS	NS	10	12	=	36	Fail
D	8	8	7	10	9	=	44	Pass

NS, work not submitted for marking.

Table 9.3 Contribution of course work and examination marks to assessment in each course unit

	Course units			
	1	2	3	4
Student W				
Course work	68	64	64	60
Examination	64	59	47	69
Total*	65	61	52	66
Student X				
Course work	62	59	63	56
Examination	32	38	39	50
Total*	41†	44	46	52
Student Y				
Course work	53	50	57	53
Examination	43	42	55	46
Total*	46	44	56	48
Student Z				
Course work	20	38	57	42
Examination	47	65	57	58
Total*	39	57	57	53

Notes   * The total for each course unit is calculated as 30% course work mark plus 70% examination mark.

† This student may fail in this unit, in spite of good course work, because the examination mark is so low.

weaker but better organized student (e.g. student D in Table 9.2) may pass. Note also that a student who obtains poor course work marks, even with satisfactory examination marks, may fail to achieve a pass in this aspect of the work (e.g. student Z in Table 9.3).

WRITING AND LEARNING

Most of your compositions at school and college (and afterwards) are prepared for other people. However, consider their value to yourself.

1. Thinking and planning, as part of active study (see p. 64) are aids to learning. You review one aspect of your work as you think and plan, deciding what should or should not be included. You recognize gaps in your knowledge and then try to fill them.
2. Each composition is a vehicle for self-expression. You will feel satisfaction when the work is complete.
3. If your work has been done thoroughly you will feel that writing has increased your understanding.
4. Compositions are required, in course work, not only as a means of monitoring your progress and assessing your work but also to give you regular practice in expressing your thoughts clearly and concisely (as you will have to do in examinations).
5. Preparing a composition helps you to view your own progress and to benefit from a reader's comments.
6. Thinking and planning encourage creative activity (see p. 105), which is a source of pleasure. You organize your thoughts and then, in writing, you present ideas and information *in your own way*. You ensure that your composition is original in approach, content and arrangement. No one else would, for example, select the same material for inclusion, make the same criticisms, decide upon the same arrangement, or reach the same conclusions.

Consider, carefully, any comments written on your marked work. Learn from these criticisms and suggestions, which are intended not only as corrections but also as advice – to help you to do better work. If you are still unable to understand any comment, after thinking carefully and consulting your notes and books, you should ask the lecturer concerned for help. Then file your marked work with your lecture notes on this aspect of your studies. To benefit further from your experience in preparing this composition, amend your lecture notes where necessary and, perhaps, revise your topic outline.

There is no harm in discussing relevant points with a fellow student before you write a composition but close collaboration is obviously unacceptable. Unless instructed to do otherwise you must always prepare your own topic outline, to ensure an original approach, and then write alone.

However, after set work has been assessed, much is to be gained by looking carefully at the work of students whose marks are higher than your own. The best of these will serve as specimen answers – indicating what is required by your teachers from students on your course. You may find that their work contains fewer mistakes, or includes only relevant information and ideas, or is better organized and more complete. Considering these differences, and any comments on your own assessed work, should help you to recognize your strengths and weaknesses and to improve your next composition.

10

Express yourself

A command of language provides the basis for learning: words help you to think and to express your thoughts. The more words you know, therefore, the better are you able to express yourself. However, communicating your thoughts unambiguously, so that you cannot be misunderstood, is not just a matter of choosing the right words.

To express yourself clearly in writing, with no help from facial expressions or other gestures, your words must be effectively arranged in sentences. This is why grammar, the art of using words correctly in an appropriate context, is important in any language.

If you plan to be a scientist or engineer, and think that clear writing and the correct use of language are more important for students of arts subjects than for you, be assured that this is not so. Scientists and engineers must be able to conduct investigations and to communicate their results. They are expected to work with precision – and communication is part of their work.

Whatever your subject, if you need help with your writing, the advice given in this chapter should help you to avoid those mistakes in the use of language that are most commonly encountered in students' written work.

WRITE IN PARAGRAPHS

Because each paragraph is concerned with one topic, your paragraphs will vary in length. However, it is probably best in course work and examinations if no paragraph is too long. If the topics in your composition are of comparable importance, your paragraphs will probably be similar in length – contributing to a balanced whole.

Effective paragraphing helps you to arrange topics in a logical order, to avoid digression, to give a complete answer, and to hold your reader's attention and interest.

In an essay-type answer your first paragraph should introduce the subject. You should normally make clear, by your use of words from the question, that you do understand what is required and that you have begun to answer the question (see p. 122). Each paragraph should be signposted by starting a new line and by indentation, and should be concerned with a distinct part of your answer (one topic). The first sentence should normally be the topic sentence which indicates clearly what the paragraph is about, and this should help you to keep to the point.

Use the first words of each paragraph to convey information: these first words make most impact upon the reader. This is especially important for a student who is trying to score marks by adding to what has already been said. However, if you think it will help your reader to see each of your main points, do number your paragraphs or use effective subheadings (as in a magazine or newspaper article). Your first words will then help you to grasp the reader's attention and to score marks.

Short answers to questions, occupying only a few pages of writing, do not normally require a summary. Additional marks cannot be given for repeating things that have already been marked. It is best to use your final paragraph to say something more. It should not be a summary but an effective conclusion that follows logically from, and draws together, your preceding paragraphs.

WRITE IN SENTENCES

Even when you are making notes it is best to use either single words and phrases, to serve as reminders, or to write concise but carefully constructed sentences. If words and punctuation marks are missing, for example from arguments, explanations or definitions, you may not be able to understand your notes when you refer to them some time later.

Similarly, in course work and examinations, readers are most likely to understand complete and properly constructed sentences. If you have difficulty in expressing thoughts clearly and simply, you are advised to write in short sentences and to use one sentence to express just one thought.

What is wrong with each of the following sentences?

1. He only made one journey which aroused the interest of detectives.
2. Only one in seven candidates is accepted because of bad spelling.
3. After the speeches . . . the two youngest boys received momentums.
4. It is my pleasure to thank the ladies who helped to serve the refreshments, which included two young girls.
5. Mrs Clay gave a demonstration on China painting, and some members painted themselves.
6. If we imagine a student on a three-year course who reads eleven hours per week during ten-week terms but never during vacations nor at any time in the rest of his life, he would need to make less than 3 per cent improvement in reading efficiency after thirty hours' tuition before we could say that the time spent training him to read faster was not saved by increased efficiency.
7. Naturally, the postal courses which have been in existence the longest must be the best, otherwise they would not have survived so long.

Some comments

1. The word 'only' is out of place. The author presumably intended to write not that *he made only one journey* but that *only one of his journeys* aroused the interest of detectives.
2. The meaning intended here is that six out of seven candidates are rejected because of their bad spelling.
3. Malopropisms, which result from confusing words that are similar in sound or spelling (e.g. momentum and momento), are named after Mrs Maloprop, a character in Sheridan's *The Rivals* who confused many words (e.g. contagious for contiguous).
4. The speaker intended to thank the ladies who, helped by two young girls, had served the refreshments.
5. Here again events are incorrectly reported as a result of lack of care in writing the sentence.

6. This sentence, with 71 words, is too long and includes clumsy phrases such as *not saved by increased*. The writer's intended meaning can be conveyed clearly, and more forcefully, in 41 words, as follows.

> In three years at college, a student who reads for eleven hours per week — in term time only — would need to improve his reading efficiency by three per cent to more than offset the thirty hours spent on a reading course.

7. Only one course can be the best. Also, the evidence given does not support the illogical statement. A new course could be the best.

TAKE AN INTEREST IN WORDS

Learning any new words, and practice in using them correctly in sentences, will improve your command of language. You are advised, therefore, to have a good dictionary on your bookshelf (see p. 174).

However, a more common fault in writing than the use of the wrong word is the use of a long word when a short one would be better (e.g. commence, fabricate, importantly, individuals and utilize – for begin, build, important, people and use); and the use of more words than are needed to convey a message pleasurably (e.g. actual facts, green in colour, and I myself would hope – for facts, green, and I hope). Superfluous words are obstacles to efficient communication and so are more than a waste of your reader's time.

Use enough words for your purpose: neither too few nor too many. Most readers will be impressed not by long words (Fig. 10.1) or by an excess of words but by relevant information and good ideas clearly and simply expressed. Just as practice enables a golfer to complete a course in fewer strokes, so practice enables a writer to develop a more direct and simple style. In golf you try to go round a course in as few strokes as possible, but the ball must be put in one hole before you can proceed to the next. Similarly, in writing practice an economy of words but use enough to convey your meaning. Also, help readers to follow your argument by making proper connections between sentences and paragraphs.

George Orwell wrote in 1950, in an essay on *Politics and the English Language*, that those who wished to use language as an instrument for expressing and not for concealing thought should:

PREFER THE SHORT WORD UNLESS A LONG WORD
WILL SERVE YOUR PURPOSE BETTER

Fig. 10.1 To be able to study at home may be an advantage depending upon your circumstances.

1. Be positive. Especially, avoid double negatives such as *not unlikely* (for *possible*) and *not unjustifiable*.
2. Never use a metaphor, simile or other figure of speech which you are used to seeing in print.
3. Never use a long word where a short one will do.
4. Never use a foreign phrase, a scientific word or a jargon word if you can think of an everyday English equivalent.
5. If it is possible to cut a word out, always cut it out.
6. Never use the passive where you can use the active.

This is still good advice for a student writing today.

Write in standard language

Although colloquial language and slang may be used in conversation, and in correspondence between close friends, they should not be used in course work and examinations (except when reporting conversations). Colloquial and slang words are marked in a dictionary by abbreviations (colloq. and sl.), so consult a dictionary if you think a word may not be acceptable in your written work.

Colloquial language includes the shortened forms of certain

words, in which missing letters are replaced by an apostrophe. In your course work and examinations prefer *do not* to *don't, will not* to *won't, cannot* to *can't*, and *it is* to *it's*.

The words used in questions

One of the most common faults in students' course work and in examinations is a failure to answer precisely the question asked. Your first step in preparing any answer in course work or in examinations, must be to consider carefully the precise wording of the question and the meaning of each word used (see p. 122). What exactly does your reader want to know?

In examinations you must allow at least a few moments for a relaxed but careful consideration of any question before you plan your answer. However, while you have time, consider the meaning of the words that are commonly used in the questions set in course work and examinations, for example:

> account, analyse, assess, brief, calculate, comment, compare, consider, contrast, criticize, define, describe, detailed, discuss, enumerate, essay, evaluate, explain, general, how, illustrate, interpret, justify, list, opinion, outline, prove, relate, review, state, summarize, trace, and view.

In advanced courses, especially, questions are set to test not only your ability to remember what you have studied but also your understanding. Therefore, you are less likely to be instructed to *describe* something than, for example, to *criticize, discuss, evaluate,* or *outline*. To do such things well you must have mastered your subject, be able to distinguish main points from supporting detail, and be willing to answer precisely the question asked. You are unlikely to be asked to write all you know about a subject. Instead the words of the question will indicate clearly just what is required. As in all writing the most important consideration is not what you would like to tell the reader but what the reader wants or needs to know (for example, see Table 10.1).

If told to discuss you must present a reasoned discussion of the evidence that bears upon the question – not unsupported opinions. If you have to explain the difference between process A and process B do not simply describe A and then B. If asked to compare things you must also contrast them. If instructed to write an essay you must do

Table 10.1 Some instructions used in questions and their meanings

Instruction	What you are expected to do
Criticize	Judge the merit of a work, person, statement, or thing. Include points in favour as well as against.
Describe	Give a description in words (and perhaps including a diagram) so that the reader can form an idea of an object, sensation, incident etc. Is your opinion required?
Discuss	Draw attention to all aspects of the question, consider different views and interpretations, and any applications.
Evaluate	Balance evidence for and against, and then give your opinion in the light of this evidence.
Illustrate	Include a diagram or give a definite example (depending upon the context).
Outline	Indicate the limits or scope of your answer; include main points only (not details). What? Where? When? How? Why? Who?

so; but understand that an answer in a written examination should not necessarily be in essay form. If asked to define a term you must give a carefully considered definition (see p. 124). If asked for *either . . . or . . .* do not do both. If asked to answer in a certain number of words, do not write more. If asked to list items, do make a list – in an appropriate order – but do no more unless another instruction indicates that more is required. If asked for an annotated diagram only, do no more.

Unless you consider carefully the meaning of each word used in a question, you are unlikely to give a complete or correct answer. As a result you will not score all the marks available. It is worth undertaking a four part analysis of any question before planning your answer (see Tables 10.2 and 10.3).

The words of your subject

Every subject has its own technical terms: the words that are peculiar to the subject, or used in a special sense.

These words are used in your textbooks but they may not be fully explained or sufficiently defined. You may have to look at more than one book to make sure that you understand the meaning of each term

Table 10.2 Thinking about the words used in a question

Question Make brief notes on the difficulties encountered in making observations; and then explain why observation is important in science.

Analysis of question

1. Subject matter
   Observation

2. Aspect of subject matter
   (i) *Difficulties*
   (ii) *Importance in science*

3. Restriction/expansion of subject matter
   Brief notes (not an essay) on difficulties
   (not on methods or other aspects)
   Why observation is important *in science*
   Note that the words of the question tell you what is required and this should cause you to omit aspects of your knowledge of the general subject area that are not relevant to this question.

4. Instructions
   Make brief notes
   then explain

Plan of answer

1. *Difficulties encountered in making observations*
   (i) *Inadequate preparation*
   (ii–v) see pp. 71–5 for subheadings.
   Write brief notes only below each subheading: enough to indicate that you do understand the difficulty.

2. *Importance of observation in science**
   (i) Science is *knowledge*: new observations are additions to knowledge.
   (ii) Scientists observe things that they do not understand; they recognize these as *problems*.
   (iii) Problems may be stated as questions; and *hypotheses* are possible answers.
   (iv) Observations made to obtain further *evidence* bearing upon the problem.
   (v) Experiments made to *test* hypotheses: observations recorded as *data*.
   (vi) Published observations may be *starting point* in work of other scientists.

---

* See Fig. 6.3, p. 67.

Table 10.3 Thinking about the words used in another question

Question Give an account of population growth in England in the
         eighteenth century.

Analysis of question

1. Subject matter
   Population

2. Aspect of subject matter
   Growth

3. Restriction/expansion of subject matter
      (i) England (not Britain or United Kingdom)
      (ii) In eighteenth century (not 17th, 19th or 20th century)
   Note that the words of the question tell you what is required and,
   therefore, remind you of what is not required.

4. Instructions
   Give an account

Plan of answer
      Population of England in 1700
                  and in 1800
      Growth of towns/rural population
      Immigration/emigration: affect on population size.
      Possible reasons for population growth in England.
      Conclusion, including reference to other countries: world
      perspective.

---

that is new to you. Unless you know these words you will be
handicapped in your studies and you may not understand some
questions in examinations.

Show your understanding of the technical terms of your subject by
using them correctly and, when you are asked to do so, by giving a
precise and complete definition.

Definitions

The best way to make yourself think about the meaning of any term
is to try to define it, correctly and completely but concisely. Also,
some examination questions start with the word define. You must
therefore, consider carefully what a definition is.

In a definition you must start by stating the general class to which
the thing to be defined belongs and then proceed to its particular
characteristics. For example, of the kinds of words used in a
language, you might start defining a noun by saying that it is a word.

It belongs to the general class of things called words. But what kind of word is it? How do you recognize a noun? You need a definition that would enable anyone to distinguish this kind of word from any other – such as a verb.

When you prepare a definition, first note the points that must be included, as if you were preparing a topic outline for an essay. Then write your definition. It should be as simple as possible and yet must cover all instances of the thing defined. Note that the definition does not include examples, but it is usually followed by an example or by examples.

> A noun is *a word that is the name of a thing*,
> such as a person, a place, an object, or an emotion.

Preparing a definition that is as simple as possible but complete and accurate, is an aid to learning. This is probably the only way for you to test that you do understand fully the words of your subject. It should be a regular part of active study.

Check your written definitions by consulting a dictionary and your textbooks. You may find, even in textbooks, that different authors give different definitions of the same term: perhaps some are incomplete. If, after thinking about a word carefully, you are not sure that your definition is correct, discuss the term with a lecturer.

Avoid abbreviations

The use of abbreviations saves time in note-taking (see Table 5.1, p. 46) but it is best to avoid abbreviations in assessed work, if you can, and to explain any necessary abbreviation (in parenthesis) the first time you use it.

Abbreviations that are so well known as to require no explanation must be used correctly. Some students indicate that they do not know the meaning of the abbreviations e.g. (L. *exempli gratia*: for example) and i.e. (L. *id est*: that is) by using one when they should be using the other.

The abbreviation etc., at the end of a list (as on p. 79), indicates only that the list is incomplete. It is usually better to write the words *including* or *for example* immediately before the list.

WRITE REGULARLY AND READ GOOD PROSE

Part of your long-term preparation for answering the kinds of questions you will be set in examinations (see p. 160), which will also result in better course work marks than could otherwise be possible, is to prepare and write answers to questions regularly throughout your course – even if homework is not set regularly.

The easiest way to overcome any reluctance to put pen to paper and to ensure regular practice in composition, is to correspond regularly with a friend or relative. This provides opportunities for self-expression, if each letter is considered and has a beginning, a paragraph for each topic, and a suitable conclusion. Pleasure comes from writing your letters and from receiving replies.

The way we speak is influenced, usually subconsciously, by the speech we hear. Similarly, our ability to write good English can be improved by reading good English regularly. Reading, also, is a source of enlightenment and pleasure. If you read a newspaper, take one that is well written, interesting, and suitable for a person of your intelligence. Also, read well-written books by authors who know how to capture your attention and maintain your interest.

WRITE LEGIBLY

Clear handwriting makes for easy communication, and so contributes to efficiency and is good manners. If a word is necessary you will want people to be able to read it. Words that cannot be read convey no meaning and so, for a student, can score no marks – but they do create an unfavourable impression. If necessary, therefore, try to improve your handwriting for *legibility and speed*.

Letters should not be so small that they are hard to read, nor so large that there is no space between the lines of writing. And the gap between words should not be so small that the words merge, nor so large that the spaces instead of the words capture the reader's attention.

With your paragraphs in mind, write in whole sentences – not thinking of one word at a time. Therefore, form letters so that each word can be written quickly. Legibility is important but a laboured neatness is more than a waste of time: slow handwriting holds back your train of thought and, if time is limited, reduces the number of thoughts that you can express.

Unlike slow reading (see p. 10), slow writing is a handicap for a student. Children learn to read one letter at a time, and in learning to write they must, of course, print each letter separately. Many slow writers continue to do this: they do not progress from printing to *real* writing. If you form each letter separately but would like to write faster, practice forming patterns, connected letters, and whole words, without lifting your pen from the page before the end of a line or the end of a word. As you write, complete each word before raising your pen from the paper to cross t's and dot i's, and to proceed quickly to the next word – until rapid writing is a habit.

Whatever you write, leave adequate margins and do not break words between lines: if there is not enough space for the whole word at the end of one line, start the word on the next.

Set yourself speed tests. Write something that you wish to learn by heart (see p. 62). Write it again and again, as a writing speed test, until you know the words. Repeat this exercise with other things that you must learn.

For all assessed work use black or blue-black ink, so that (i) there is sufficient contrast between your words and the page, and (ii) your writing cannot be confused with the markers' comments and corrections.

11

Working on a special study

A special study, involving an investigation or survey and a project report, or the preparation of a term paper or extended essay, may be a major part of your final year's work. The marks awarded will probably affect your final grade (e.g. see Table 11.1).

Because the special study provides opportunities for challenging, interesting and independent work, and to score marks outside the examinations, do not make the common mistake of devoting too much time to it. If you do, you may obtain a good mark for the special study but at the expense of poorer marks for other work (see marks of student V in Table 11.1). You are therefore advised to relate the amount of time you devote to the special study to its importance, in relation to other course units. For example, if one fifth of the marks available in the final year come from each course unit and one fifth from the special study (see Table 11.1), you should allocate about one fifth of your study time to each of these aspects of your work.

SELECTING A SUBJECT FOR YOUR SPECIAL STUDY

Agree the title and scope of the work proposed with your supervisor. You will need your supervisor's advice about what you can be expected to accomplish in the time available (see Table 11.4). Also, look at satisfactory compositions completed by other students in previous years of your course, to get an idea of what they were able to accomplish – but do not be impressed by their length and make sure

Table 11.1 Contribution of marks for special study and marks for other course units, to the final mark upon which a student's grade is based

	Course units					
	1	2	3	4	5 (Special study)	Final mark
Student V	41	53	41	45	68	50
Student W	65	61	52	66	80	65
Student X	41	44	46	52	55	48
Student Y	46	44	56	48	52	49
Student Z	39	57	57	53	42	50

that you do not exceed the number of words required.

Choose a subject in which you are already interested and which will complement and support your other studies. Either you or your supervisor should write concise *terms of reference* which state, as precisely as is possible at this stage, what you are required to do. These may have to be modified later, in the light of experience, with your supervisor's agreement. They should be neither too wide (so that all relevant sources of information could not be consulted in the time available) nor too narrow (dealing with a subject about which little has been published). Apart from the collection of material for inclusion, a major composition is required, which will probably be longer than any you have previously undertaken.

It is best to restrict any investigation to a particular aspect of the subject that will interest not only yourself but also your readers. However, it is probably best to avoid aspects about which you feel so strongly that you would find it difficult to produce a balanced composition.

Establish, at the outset, that any essential publications, equipment or materials will be available when you need them and for as long as you may need them.

ASSESSING A SPECIAL STUDY

All students taking a particular course will undertake special studies on different aspects of their subject – in contrast to other course work in which all students answer the same question. In these extended exercises the students use different methods and have

YOUR COMPOSITION IS ALL THAT SOME
ASSESSORS WILL SEE

Fig. 11.1   A common mistake is to attempt too much, and to neglect other work.

different supervisors, and differ in both their need for advice and in the amount of help they receive. All these differences must be considered by supervisors and examiners if each student's work is to be fairly assessed.

Clearly, you need to know how your composition is to be presented and how the work as a whole will be assessed. Marks are likely to be given for the way you approach and plan the work; for the thoroughness with which you gather and analyse data, and interpret the results; for initiative and originality; for your ability to relate your findings to the work of others; and for your ability to select relevant material and present this in a clear, concise and well organized extended essay or project report.

Your composition should therefore indicate, as appropriate, not only what you have done but also your approach to the problems involved, to the interpretation of work done by others, and to the analysis and interpretation of any new observations. Because of all these things, as in all other assessed work, what you write and how well you write will play a major part in the assessment of your work. Remember that, apart from your supervisor, unless there is an oral examination, your composition is the assessor's only guide to the quality of your work (Fig. 11.1).

WORKING ON YOUR OWN

In a special study you work on your own but with your supervisor's advice when you need it (Table 11.2). You will have to gather information and organize your material before writing the essay or report. You may also collect original data – by observation alone, by observation and experiment, by interview or other survey methods, or by correspondence (see also Chapter 5).

Keep your supervisor informed of the way your work is going, but look upon the special study as an opportunity to work effectively on your own, to gather information from different sources, to assess its value in relation to your work, to show your knowledge of the subject, to organize and communicate the results of your thinking, and to complete the work on time.

Table 11.2 Working, with supervision, on a special study

Activities	
Choosing a title Writing terms of reference	With supervisor
Finding information Gathering data	Ask supervisor for advice when necessary.
Selecting Analysing Ordering Interpreting Summarizing	Keep supervisor informed of progress.
Drafting report	Let supervisor see draft.
Revising report	Consider any comments.
Rewriting report	

REPORTING YOUR WORK

The students taking a particular course are likely to be given written instructions or *Notes for Guidance*:

1. To help them with their writing.
2. To encourage uniformity.
3. To make for easy reading.
4. To facilitate marking.

These notes will indicate a maximum number of words to be used (or for a typed report a maximum number of pages), when the composition is to be submitted for assessment, and how the work is to be presented (see p. 139).

A project based on reading, with no supporting personal observations, will be written as an extended essay or review. As in any other essay, you will include an introduction and conclusion but the body of your essay will comprise many paragraphs. These must be arranged in a logical order, and you will help yourself and your readers if you group closely related paragraphs below appropriate headings and subheadings. You must therefore plan your report, just as you would any other composition.

If a project involves the collection and analysis of data, as well as the study of relevant published work, the project report may be arranged as in Table 11.3. Using the accepted headings, and knowing the kind of information placed by convention below each heading, makes writing easier and helps the readers to find answers to their questions: Who? When? Where? What? Why? How?

Another type of project, preparing an instruction manual, may be appropriate in some courses. This manual may be arranged as follows: Cover; Title page; Acknowledgements; List of contents; Description of equipment; Operating instructions; Maintenance instructions; Servicing instructions; Fault-finding and fault-correction. In preparing instructions, as in all except imaginative writing, the essential characteristics are explanation, clarity, simplicity, completeness, accuracy, and good order. Each step should be distinct, and preferably it should be numbered, so that you know that you have completed one step before you start the next.

In other courses, a suitable project might be the preparation of a guide to the organization and work of an agency, institution, firm or service. Such a project report might be arranged as follows: Cover; Title page; Acknowledgements; List of contents; Introduction (including the reasons for the existence of the agency, institution etc., and the purpose of the project report); Method of enquiry (including how you obtained the information presented in your report, and what problems you encountered); Results (of your enquiry); Conclusions; Summary; Sources of information; Appendices.

If you are familiar with appropriate learned journals you will know how authors usually present their work in your subject, and how sources of information or ideas are usually acknowledged. This

Table 11.3 The parts of a project report

Part	Content
Cover sheet	Full title. Your name. Course title. Name of your college. Date.
Title page	Full title. Your name.
Acknowledgements	Who helped? In what way did they help? Mention only your supervisor and anyone who helped materially with your work. Do not use flowery language. For a typed report it is not necessary to name the typist.
List of contents	List of headings and subheadings used in your composition, with page numbers. In a short work this list may not be necessary.
Introduction	Why did you do this work? What was the problem? State your terms of reference. State briefly how this study is related to the work of others. Refer to things that you expect all your readers to know and build on this foundation: proceed from the general (subject area) to the particular (one aspect), or from the whole to its parts. In this way, give your readers a framework upon which the information and ideas presented in your composition can be hung. If a *Literature survey* is required, include this at the end of the *Introduction* after a subheading.
Materials and methods	What materials did you use? How did you carry out your investigation? The purpose of this section is not only to inform but also to enable a reader to repeat the work and obtain similar data.
Results	State your findings simply and clearly. You may include diagrams and tables in which the results of your analysis of data are presented.
Discussion	What do you make of your results? How do they relate to the work of others – especially those mentioned in your *Introduction*. Do not express opinions as if they were facts, and do not present other people's opinions as if they were your own.
Conclusions	List your conclusions, which should follow logically from the *Results* and *Discussion* sections. Are you able to answer any of the questions raised in your *Introduction*? *Recommendations* may be listed at the end of this section, below a subheading.
Summary	What are your main findings? Be sure to include

Table 11.3 *Continued*

Part	Content
	anything original, any achievements, and anything else you particularly want the examiners to know about. The summary may be placed after the *Conclusions*, as indicated here, or immediately before the *Introduction*.
List of references	In your *Introduction*, *Materials and methods*, and *Discussion* sections, cite only publications that you have consulted. And in your list of references, give full bibliographic details (see p. 48 and p. 175) for every publication cited but for no others.
Appendices	Tables of data, summarized in your *Results* section, may be included in an *Appendix*. Other relevant material that would be out of place in the body of your report may be included in other appendices, if your supervisor agrees that this would be appropriate.

may be done, for example, by inserting numbers (in parentheses) in the composition, corresponding to the numbers used in a list of references. Alternatively, the author's name may be included in the composition (followed immediately by the date of publication of the work in parenthesis) and again full bibliographic details are given in a list of sources.

In arts subjects, works that have influenced your thinking or approach, indirectly, as a result of your background reading, may be included in a *Bibliography* at the end of your composition (instead of the *List of references* given in scientific and technical reports).

Whatever your subject, you will find it helpful to look at satisfactory compositions prepared by students who have completed the course you are taking.

Starting to write

Plan all parts of your special study. Allocate time to thinking, to collecting information, and to planning, writing and revising your composition (see Table 11.4). Start early and be determined to complete the work on time so that you can concentrate on other work in the last six to eight weeks before your final examinations (see p. 149).

For example

June/July	Agree title and terms of reference with your supervisor.
Aug/Dec	Survey literature, read relevant articles and selected passages from books, and collect data.
Dec/Jan	Complete first draft of composition.
Feb/Mar	Revise composition and have it typed.
April	Check composition and submit it for assessment.
May/June	Complete final revision of other aspects of work for final examinations.

Do not spend so much time on reading that you have no time to collect data, and do not spend so much time collecting data that you have no time to write.

Also, do not complete your investigations and then start to write. Unlike other compositions prepared for homework and in examinations, this longer composition is unlikely to be written at one sitting. It is best to look upon writing as an aid to thinking and planning, and to prepare your extended essay, project report, or term paper, throughout the time available for the work (see Table 11.4).

Plan your composition and select appropriate section headings at the beginning. Select subsection headings as soon as possible, so that you can collect and file material under them. At this stage, use your topic outline as a contents page.

Write each paragraph on a separate sheet of A4 paper and use words from the topic sentence as a heading on this sheet. Then write on one side of the sheet only. This will help you to say all that you wish to say on each topic in one place, to move material that would be irrelevant in this place, and to add paragraphs later in the most appropriate places.

You should be able to write a brief and concise first draft of the *Introduction*, including your terms of reference (see p. 129) as soon as you have decided what you are going to do and why this seems to be worth doing. You can write your *Methods* section as soon as you have decided how to collect information in your investigation. Data can be collected, recorded on data sheets, and analysed, and the results summarized, as your work proceeds, so that all the necessary information is ready when you come to prepare the *Results* section.

Notes can also be made, throughout your work, of points that you think may be included in the *Discussion*. In this way, the parts of the first draft can be written in more or less the right order.

You will also find it helpful to record the complete bibliographic details of each reference consulted during your literature survey and in your further or background reading, on a separate index card (see p. 58).

If you work in this way you will have regular practice in writing and the first draft of your composition should be complete at about the same time as your investigations (see Table 11.4). Another advantage of writing in this way is that, if necessary, you can check your work while any equipment or sources of information, needed for the work, are still available and there is still time.

Table 11.4 Allocation of time to a project:
6 hours each week for 22 weeks

Note Each symbol represents one hour's work.

```
1 2 3 4 5 6 7 8 9 10 11   vacation   12 13 14 15 16 17 18 19 20 21 22 vacatio

1
1 1
1 1 1
1 1 1 1
1 1 1 1 1   1   1          1                1         1         1
Literature search/reading


                d                        d
      d d d d d   d   d          d   d   d
      d d d d d   d   d          d   d   d       d
      d d d d d   d   d          d   d   d   d   d   d   d
      d d d d d   d   d          d   d   d   d   d   d   d
      d d d d d   d   d          d   d   d   d   d   d   d
      Collecting data


                                                          r   r   t   t
                                                          r   r   t   t
                                                          r   r   t   t
    w                       w w w                    w    r   r   t   t
  w w                       w w w          w w w w w      r   r   t   t
w w w       w     w         w w w        w w w w w w      r   r   t   t
Writing report                                          Revising
                                                        and typing
                                                           report
```

Preparing diagrams and tables

Remember that, in addition to writing, you will need time to prepare diagrams and tables. Each of these should be planned so that it fits upright on the page, and should occupy a separate sheet of paper unless you wish to facilitate comparison. There should be an appropriate legend (below each figure) or heading (above each table), as in this book. Diagrams and tables should be numbered, separately, so that you can refer to them in any part of your composition.

Make sure that you do refer to each diagram and to each table, at least once, in your composition. You should need fewer words in the text because information presented in a diagram or table should not be repeated in the text. Nor should information be presented in both a diagram and a table: convey your message clearly and once only.

Writing for your readers

Remember, in preparing any communication, that it is not enough to write something that you can understand. This is especially important when you are reporting on work in which you have been involved for some time. You should be closer to the investigation, and therefore more familiar with your material, than your readers. In starting to read, they are at the beginning of your investigation, whereas you are at the end.

All reports have both primary readers (those who asked for the report and who may make a decision or take action on the basis of the report) and secondary readers (who receive the report for information only and who read only the title and, perhaps, the *Introduction*, *Conclusions*, and *Summary*). Primary readers (who may know almost as much as you do about your project) may be expected to read the whole report and to understand every sentence. Secondary readers of a project report are those who are experts on other subjects but who are unlikely to be as well informed as your supervisor (or yourself) on the subject considered in your composition. Write for your primary readers in the first place, and then make sure that your *Introduction, Conclusions*, and *Summary*, at least, could be understood by a secondary reader.

In all parts of a report your meaning should be expressed as simply and clearly as possible, and technical terms should be either avoided if they might not be understood by some secondary readers or sufficiently explained when they are first used.

Consider your readers. Who are they? Your supervisor is closest to the work; the second internal assessor is unlikely to be a specialist in the same area of work; and you do not know the external assessor's interests.

Whenever you speak or write, try to express yourself not only in words that you understand but also in a way that will be understood by others. This is not an easy task, but you are unlikely to communicate effectively unless you consider the needs of your audience.

CHECKING AND TYPING

Check your completed composition

1. Have you followed any instructions or *Notes for Guidance*?
2. Are the cover and title pages complete (see Table 11.3)?
3. Does the title provide the best concise description of the contents of your composition?
4. Is the *List of Contents* necessary? Check, if it is, that all your headings and subheadings are arranged in the same order and worded in the same way as in the text.
5. Does each part of the report start with a main heading at the top of a page?
6. Is everything in the composition relevant to the title and to the preceding heading?
7. Have you kept to the terms of reference (see p. 129) and are these clearly stated in your *Introduction*?
8. Do your main points stand out?
9. Is every paragraph, sentence, and word, necessary? Anything superfluous will distract attention from your message.
10. Is anything repeated? To avoid repetition, if a reminder is needed, include a cross reference (as in point 7, above).
11. Has anything essential been omitted?
12. Is each statement accurate and based on sufficient evidence; and are all your sources properly acknowledged?
13. Are your arguments arranged logically and your conclusions clearly stated, and is anything original emphasized sufficiently?
14. Are any tables and diagrams correctly numbered, on separate sheets, and referred to in appropriate places in the text?

15. Is any information presented in a table repeated in a diagram or, unnecessarily, in the text?
16. Are any technical terms, symbols or abbreviations sufficiently explained?
17. Are there any words such as *many* or *few* which should be replaced by numbers?
18. Are there any mistakes, including mistakes in grammar or spelling?
19. Is the composition as a whole well balanced?
20. Does the revised report look neat and does it sound well when read aloud?

It is a good idea to ask someone, who has not been closely connected with your work, to read your composition to see if they can find any obvious mistakes, any unnecessary technical terms, or any sentences that are not clearly expressed. Also your supervisor may like to see your corrected first draft.

Consider any suggestions and then, if necessary, revise your composition. Even if your report is to be typed, you will need to make sure that it is legible and neatly set out for the typist – with any instructions about arrangement and presentation stated clearly.

Typing

If you cannot obtain *Notes for Guidance* or precise instructions, on presentation, look at similar compositions completed by students in the previous years of your course. The typist will require detailed instructions, such as the following.

1. Use A4 paper.
2. Include separate cover and title pages; and a list of contents.
3. Start each main heading at the top of a new sheet. Centre main headings but not subheadings. Type each table on a separate sheet.
4. Leave a 40 mm margin on the left and a 25 mm margin on the right, top and bottom of the page.
5. Use a standard type face (not italics) and type in double-spacing on one side of each sheet only.
6. Number all pages, except the cover, title, and contents pages, in Arabic numerals, at the top right hand corner.
7. Keep a copy.

Before handing your manuscript to the typist, check that you have used capital letters or underlined words only where you require them, that the whole composition is set out according to your requirements, and that the exact position of each figure and table is indicated.

12

Preparing for examinations

Your performance in examinations, and perhaps also in assessed course work (see p. 112 and p. 128), determines your progress through the course and your final result. Your purpose in study, therefore, will be not only to master your subjects but also to do as well as possible in both course work and examinations.

CONSIDER WHAT IS EXPECTED OF YOU

One of the main causes of under-achievement at college is the student's failure to understand just what is required in a particular course. Apart from good organization, a sustained and well directed effort is required. An understanding of what is expected in your course may be derived from:

1. Your lecture notes which, with the course outline and syllabus, indicate the scope of the work upon which you will be examined.
2. Your textbooks and other recommended reading.
3. The questions set in previous years' examination papers.
4. The exercises set in class and for homework.
5. The comments upon, and the marks awarded for, your course work.

In assessed course work, always try to learn from any comments or corrections (see p. 114); and always try to read the work of other students who have scored higher marks than you (see p. 115). You can then see not only where you went wrong but also how other people convey information and ideas more completely and more effectively than you do.

If, after looking through your own work (and that of other students), you still do not see where you went wrong, or if you do not understand any comments or corrections written on your work, make a point of asking the marker for advice or help, just as you would ask a lecturer for help if you did not understand any point made in a lecture.

For many courses, students are given a course booklet when they arrive at college. This may include a list of the names of academic staff, a course outline, the syllabus for the course, and information about homework, examinations and assessment. Alternatively, information may be available in the college library, or may be displayed on notice boards, or individual lecturers may introduce themselves and outline what they will be teaching. Ask the Departmental Secretary, the lecturer concerned, or your personal tutor, if you do not have all the information you require. You need information on all these aspects of your work at the beginning of the course.

Also find out if there are any committees (e.g. course committees and staff–student liaison committees) on which students are represented. Talk to your elected representatives on such committees if there is any matter relating to the course that you consider should be discussed.

Always do homework, even if the marks given will not contribute to the grade awarded at the end of your course (see p. 113). Undertaking set work regularly provides valuable practice. The marks given indicate the value of each piece of work and are a guide to your progress. And any comments or corrections, if considered carefully, should help you to do better work next time. In this way your final grade will be affected indirectly, even if the marks scored in course work do not contribute directly, because you will be able to complete better answers in your final examinations.

Good study techniques, as recommended in this book, are an aid to effective study. However, flexibility is needed. Different techniques will be used on different occasions. Different subjects, different lecture courses, different lecturers, and different methods of assessment, all make different demands – and an intelligent student should be able to respond in different ways.

USE APPROPRIATE TEXTBOOKS

Some students use school textbooks as a basis for more advanced studies at college. This is usually a mistake. Your lecture notes should provide a foundation, and you should build on this by making regular and frequent use of the textbooks recommended for your present course. For further information and for background reading, get into the habit of looking at more than one source to get different opinions and approaches.

Some students consult out-of-date textbooks and reference books. However, remember that you cannot expect to obtain an up-to-date account of a subject from a book written many years ago. Always look at the date of publication and try to obtain the latest revision of each book you consult (see p. 80).

LOOK AT THE SYLLABUS

Before applying for a course you should have seen an outline of the whole course, so that you know what choice of subjects, if any, is available. Then, at the start of each year, look at the current syllabus for the examinations you will be taking. This will give a good indication of what you will be studying during the year, as well as indicating the scope of the examinations, and will help you to see the course in perspective, week by week.

It is a good idea to copy each part of the syllabus on a separate sheet of paper and to file this at the start of your notes on the subject. Remember, however, that your best and only complete guide to the course content should be your record, in your own notes, made in lectures, tutorials, and other classes, throughout the course.

The syllabus and your lecture notes provide a foundation for your further studies (see p. 45). They should set limits to your studies, so that you are not easily side-tracked into some aspects whilst others are neglected, but these limits should not be so rigid as to discourage independent thought and enquiry.

LOOK AT RECENT EXAMINATION PAPERS

Obtain copies of the examination papers for the last two years, taken by students who followed the same course. Two year's question papers will usually be enough. If you go too far back you may waste

time looking at papers set when the syllabus was different and set by
different examiners.

Look to see which aspects of the subject are examined on each
examination paper; and if any papers are divided into parts note
which aspects are examined in each part.

Past question papers are your only guide to the *arrangement* of
questions on the paper and to the *kind of choice* of question that has
to be made. The instructions at the head of the paper may state, for
example, that you must answer question one and three others, or
that you must answer at least one question from each section. You
may also be advised to devote a certain proportion of your time to
one particular question, or to one part of the paper.

Similarly, recent question papers are a guide to the *kinds of
questions* that are likely to be set. Sometimes the first question is
compulsory. You may find that there is always one question with
many parts, each requiring a short answer. Another question may
provide much of the information you need for a complete answer: if
you read it carefully before preparing your answer. Some questions
may be structured, indicating clearly the parts of your answer (e.g.
the subheadings to be used). Others may require essay-type answers.
If particular kinds of question have been set for the last two years,
you may expect a similar balance of questions in your examinations.

PLAN ANSWERS TO EXAMINATION QUESTIONS

It is a good idea to copy each question, from the last two years'
examination papers, at the top of a separate sheet of notepaper,
leaving space for a plan of your answer. Then file each question with
your revision notes on the subject.

Planning answers to examination questions helps you to recall
what you know and to reorganize your thoughts in the form of an
answer to the question asked. It will help you to think, to recognize
gaps in your knowledge or understanding, and to learn, and so is part
of active study. Try to work things out for yourself, first, but discuss
any question with a lecturer if you are not sure of its precise meaning,
or if you are not sure what is required in the answer, or if you think
that your plan may be incomplete or otherwise incorrect.

Planning answers to the kinds of questions that are likely to be set
in your examinations is good practice. You are also advised to write
out some answers in full.

In some weeks throughout the course your set work will involve answering questions similar to those set in examinations. In other weeks set yourself questions. There is no better preparation for examinations than completing answers to suitable questions in the amount of time that would be available in an examination – even if you devote more time to thinking about and planning your answer.

If there is to be a change in the kinds of questions set, the arrangement of questions on the paper, the kinds of choice to be made, or the aspects of the subject to be examined on each paper, then candidates should be told about the change well before the examinations. They should be given examples of the new kinds of questions, or specimen examination papers to illustrate the new format.

PREPARE REVISION AIDS FROM YOUR NOTES

Notes made when you are thinking or reading should be combined with your lecture notes on the same subject – so that you have only one set of notes (see Fig. 8.2, p. 89).

Nevertheless, you are likely to find as the course of study proceeds that your notes are becoming too bulky. Your notes, for all the subjects you are taking in examinations, will probably be too long to read in the few weeks preceding examinations. They may be suitable for reference but not for revision.

MAKE SHORT REVISION NOTES – PERHAPS ON INDEX CARDS

Fig. 12.1   Your notes will probably be so long that you could not read them in the last few weeks before an examination.

In earlier revision periods, therefore, throughout the course, you are advised to make shorter revision notes, from your notes, on each aspect of your work (Fig. 12.1). These concentrated revision notes should be:

Lists of basic ideas.
Concise summaries.
Topic outlines.
Annotated diagrams, and . . .
Definitions that you must remember.

Each diagram, definition, list, summary, or outline, should be on one side of a sheet of paper or, preferably, on one side of an index card (or postcard) for quick reference and for rapid but frequent reading. File these cards, in a card index, but always have a few in your pocket and study them on bus and train journeys, while you are waiting for appointments, and whenever you have a few moments to spare for private study. These cards will be invaluable in the weeks before examinations when you must revise each subject as a whole.

Annotated diagrams may be very useful revision aids – helping you, for example, to visualize a pattern or sequence of events. Include diagrams in your notes as aids to learning and revision: visualizing the whole will help you to recall the parts. Also, if appropriate, prepare simpler diagrams that could be reproduced quickly and neatly if you decided to include them in an examination answer (see Figs 12.2 and 12.3) to convey information, reduce the number of words needed in a description or explanation, and save time.

Preparing revision aids, because it makes you think again about each aspect of your work and concentrate on essentials, is in itself an effective revision technique. Having prepared a revision note on any subject you will find that you have fixed many things that you wished to learn in your mind.

You look, think, select, arrange, and write or draw – and this active study aids concentration. In preparing concise summaries of your earlier work you see connections with your later work, and this increases your understanding. You also learn by reorganizing your early work in the light of your further experience of the subject, of making notes, and of the kinds of records that you require.

TEST YOURSELF

If you sit reading notes, just trying to remember them, you may find concentration difficult and may remember very little. Furthermore, memorizing is not enough: most questions test both your knowledge and your understanding. Throughout your course, therefore, it is best to devote revision periods – like other study periods – to different kinds of activity. Consider what you need to know about each aspect of your work. Then set yourself definite tasks.

1. *Set* yourself questions of different kinds, that could be set in your examinations: analyse, define, explain etc. (see p. 121).
2. *Solve* any problems, from your textbooks, that you have not tackled previously.
3. *Organize* your knowledge of a subject – as you would before giving a lecture to next year's students taking the same course.
4. *Make* notes of any gaps in your knowledge and then, at the next opportunity, try to fill these gaps.
5. *Prepare* a topic outline for a question set earlier in the course, then compare this with the answer you wrote at the time. Could you write a better answer now?
6. *Prepare* simple diagrams from memory and then compare these with similar diagrams prepared previously.
7. *Recall* the main points on one aspect of a subject. Make notes and then compare them with your concentrated notes (see p. 145).
8. *Read* your concentrated notes repeatedly, especially in the last weeks preceding an examination.
9. *Write* definitions, from memory, then check these against your revision notes or textbook.

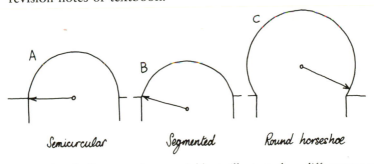

Fig. 12.2 Simple diagrams, drawn quickly, to illustrate three different types of arches used by architects.

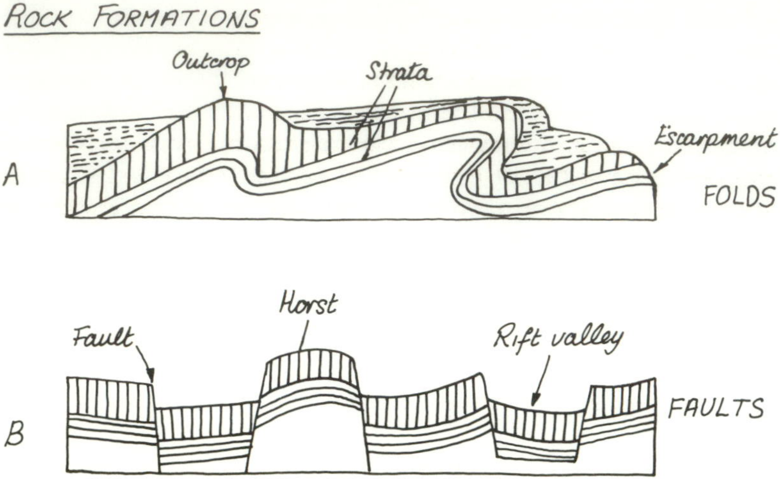

ROCK FORMATIONS

Fig. 12.3 Simple diagrams, drawn quickly and annotated to facilitate the definition of terms used in describing geological features.

PLAN YOUR REVISION

Revision is not something that can be left until the last few weeks immediately before an examination. It is part of active study.

The years before an examination

Most of the time, at college, you will be occupied with current work or looking forward to what you are about to do next, but the last part of every study period should be devoted to review and revision. You should also allocate some study periods, every week, to revision (see p. 61 and p. 68) particularly at weekends and in vacations.

Revision (looking again) starts soon after each lecture, preferably on the same evening, when you check your notes (see p. 54). Even if you are not consciously trying to remember, thinking again will help you to understand and will help to stop you forgetting! Similarly, each private study session should end with a quick review of your work in that session and with revision (see, for example, p. 87).

Regular short periods of revision will help you to remember. Revising things that you have already learned is called over-learning by psychologists: this is a method for fixing things in your mind. However revision is not simply a matter of memorizing each aspect of your work. Each time you look again at past work, you not only think about each topic again but also see it in the light of your further experience of the subject as a whole. As you work on your notes (see p. 52 and p. 89) you think more about a subject and understand it better. Furthermore, between periods of revision, you think about your subjects, assimilate information, and see connections between different aspects of your work. In this way you learn many things without the conscious effort of trying to remember them.

Regular revision (see Table 6.1, p. 61) helps you to understand past work, to cope better with current work, and to approach examinations with confidence.

The weeks before an examination

For your final revision you will probably devote more time than usual to study: perhaps working 56 hours each week instead of 49 hours (see p. 25). But continue to allocate enough time to recreation and sleep in the weeks preceding your examinations. After even a short period of recreation you will feel refreshed and ready to return to active study; and a good night's sleep will help you to avoid undue anxiety and to concentrate on your work.

Remember that in revision you should be looking at things again in the light of the course as a whole. You should be checking for accuracy and completeness, concentrating on essentials, and refreshing your memory. *You should not be learning things for the first time*. Do not miss organized classes towards the end of your course in order to spend the time on revision. These last classes may prove to be most useful. The lecturer may emphasize important points, draw conclusions, and sum up at the end of the course.

If your study time has been well organized, so that your thoughts are well organized, you will have a good set of revision notes. Your final revision will be much easier and much more effective than would otherwise be possible.

Start your final revision in good time – say eight weeks before the first examination (Table 12.1). Work to a timetable so that you are in control and you do not waste time at the start of each study session, deciding what to do. Revise each subject over the whole revision period. Do not revise one subject at a time: if you do you may run out of time and fail to revise some aspects of your work.

Make a note of the times and locations of all your examinations in

Table 12.1 Example of a plan of work for the eight weeks preceding an examination*

Weeks	Activities
8	Survey the course as a whole, as indicated by the syllabus and your notes made in class. Look at examination papers for the last two years. Consider which aspects require most attention in your revision.
7–6	Look through all your notes, checking that you have a complete set of revision notes.
5–4	Memorize revision notes. Write out revision notes from memory.
3	Prepare topic outlines and write complete answers to some questions. Memorize revision notes.
2	Set yourself a test paper, including questions you think may be set in your examination. Answer this in the time that will be allowed in your examination, then compare your answers with topic outlines prepared previously. Assess your own work. Read selected passages, on which you think you are likely to be examined, from textbooks. Memorize your revision notes.
1	Set yourself another test paper. Assess your work. Look through all your revision notes again to refresh your memory.

* Prepare your own revision plan to suit your needs.

your diary, as soon as the examinations' timetable is available.

In looking at past examination papers you may see that questions are set nearly every year on certain topics. Also, from the emphasis placed on certain aspects of your work (the amount of time devoted to them in organized classes) you may think that questions are likely to be set on these aspects. Most students try to guess which questions are likely to be included in their examinations. However, it is best to master each subject and to revise all aspects of your work so that it does not matter too much if some of your favourite topics are not examined. In taking examinations you should not be taking chances.

There are other dangers in trying to spot questions (guessing which questions are likely to be set). Some students prepare answers to these questions so that they can let the words flow forth in the examination, like a dam bursting. This is a complete waste of time if the question is not on the examination paper. And it is almost a complete waste of time if the question set is not quite the same as expected – so that a different answer is needed. The prepared answer will not do.

It is best to prepare topic outlines for the different kinds of questions that you are likely to be asked, so that in the examination you can consider the actual question set and then prepare an appropriate topic outline immediately before you start to write.

Questions may be set on all the things that you have been taught. And you will be expected, especially in advanced courses, to demonstrate in your answers that you have studied the subject yourself. As a result of observing, reading, and thinking, you should know more than you have been taught.

13

Taking examinations

The use of effective study and revision techniques should help you to gain confidence as your experience, and your knowledge and understanding of your subjects, increase. In this sense, all course work is a preparation for examinations.

The best way to avoid anxieties about course work or examinations, and to ensure that you obtain grades that are a true reflection of your ability, is to have a positive attitude to life at college. Having studied and revised subjects in which you are interested, you should be well prepared. Each examination will then be a challenge and an opportunity to display your knowledge, reasoning ability, and understanding.

Hysteria, prior to an examination, which is likely to affect performance adversely, indicates a lack of confidence which may be due to a lack of well directed effort throughout the course, followed by too much work and too little recreation in the last few weeks preceding the examinations.

Having prepared to the best of your ability, you should not feel over-anxious. But you should be keyed-up and ready for action, as an athlete would be immediately before a race – after months of preparation.

As a student you should have a desire to learn, but examinations are an additional incentive. Each examination passed provides encouragement and satisfaction, confirming that you have reached a certain standard. However, many students do not do as well as they could in examinations. Sometimes this is because they have not worked hard enough and *do not know as much about their subjects as they should*. Sometimes it is because, although they have worked hard, they have not organized their study time effectively; and sometimes they have worked hard, organized their studies, know their subjects, and yet have not thought enough about examination technique.

LEARN FROM OTHER STUDENTS' MISTAKES

(a) Master your subjects

The most common reason for failure in examinations is inadequate preparation. To master all subjects, you need to develop your interest in them (see Chapter 1); keep fit for study (Chapters 2 and 3); use your time effectively and concentrate during hours of study (Chapter 4); study effectively (Chapters 5 to 9); develop your ability to use language effectively (Chapter 10); and revise your work regularly throughout the course (Chapter 12).

(b) Select questions as directed in the instructions at the head of the question paper

Some candidates fail to answer compulsory questions – and can therefore score no marks for them. They cannot make good this omission by answering extra questions from other parts of the paper. Such extra questions will not be marked.

Some candidates when asked, for example, to answer four questions and to answer at least one from each of the sections of the paper A, B and C, answer no questions from one section. They can score no marks, therefore, for this section. And the examiner will mark only three questions from the other sections, even if four have been answered.

(c) Select questions carefully

Some candidates do not read the whole paper before deciding which questions to answer.

If an examination paper comprises many questions, each requiring only a short answer, and if all questions are to be answered, then it is probably best to start at the beginning and to work through to the end. Each question can be read, understood, considered, and a short answer recorded. Any question that is not answered immediately can be reconsidered later.

However, most advanced examinations are not of this kind. If there is a choice, you must allow a proportion of the time available for reading all the questions carefully. Consider what is required in each answer before deciding which you can answer best. If you do not do this, you may find, after completing the examination, that you could have made a better choice and scored higher marks.

(d) Answer the required number of questions

Some candidates do not answer the required number of questions. The marks allocated to each question may be indicated on the examination paper. Otherwise, the same number of marks will be available for each question. For example, if four questions have to be answered this means that up to twenty five marks could be scored for each question. If a student attempts five questions, only the first four answers will be marked: no marks will be given for the fifth answer. To answer more than the required number of questions is a waste of time – and it reduces the time you can devote to answers that will be marked. On the other hand, students who answer only three or two questions, when they should answer four, will be marked out of seventy five and fifty, respectively.

You must do your best to answer the right number of questions. However, if you find that you are unable to do this, do your best to cope with the situation: *keep your head*. If you should answer four questions but can answer only three, work steadily at these three questions and you may still score high marks. And if you can answer only two you may still pass the examination. You should also be able to score some marks by giving incomplete answers to some questions. If necessary, do this to make up the number of answers required.

(e) Allocate your time according to the marks available

Some candidates spend too much time on some questions, so that they cannot spend enough on others. They may even find that they have no time for their last answer. Make sure that you know how much time is allowed for the whole examination: then divide your time wisely. The instructions at the head of the paper may include advice about how much time should be spent on each part of the paper.

If the marks available for a question (or for the parts of a question) are stated on the paper, next to the question, this also indicates how you should allocate your time.

If the questions carry equal marks try to allocate your time equally between them (see Table 13.1). Resist the temptation to spend more time on those questions that you feel you can answer best (see Table 13.2). Remember that it is easier to score a few marks on a question that you at first felt you did not know much about (see p. 68) than to score a few extra marks by spending extra time on what is already a good answer.

Table 13.1 Allocating your time in examination

Time allowed for examination	Number of questions to be answered	Available for each question	
		Time*	Marks
180 min	6	30 min	16.7
	5	36 min	20
	4	45 min	25
	3	60 min	33.3

* Deduct from the time available for each question, the time needed for reading all the questions, deciding which questions to answer, and checking your answers.

Table 13.2 Three ways of allocating your time in a three-hour written examination, and the possible consequences

Question	Time allocation	Marks	Time allocation	Marks	Time allocation	Marks
1	55 min	16*	55 min	16*	36 min	14
2	50 min	14	50 min	14	36 min	13
3	40 min	11	40 min	11	36 min	12
4	35 min	11	20 min	8	36 min	11
5		0	15 min	6	36 min	10*
Totals		52		55		60

* In a written answer it is difficult to score more than sixteen out of twenty for a good answer, and it is relatively easy to score half marks by attending carefully to a question that you at first thought you did not know much about.

If you spend fifty minutes on a question that should be answered in thirty six, you are probably including irrelevant material, or padding; or saying the same thing twice (perhaps using different words); or giving unnecessary detail, extra examples, or more explanation than is necessary.

If you do find that you are running out of time, towards the end of an examination, it is better to write a good topic outline for a complete answer or to answer the question in note-form, than to leave a question unanswered or to write only the first parts of an answer that you do not have time to complete.

(f) Answer precisely the question asked not a slightly different question that you expected

Some candidates prepare, during their revision, an answer to a question set in a previous year and that they think may be set this year. Then they write their prepared answer in the examination – even though the question set is not identical with the one they expected. That is to say, they fail to respond to the exact wording of the question, (see p. 121). The result, at best, is that they cannot score full marks. At worst, they may write at length, including some things that would have been relevant if they had been presented as an answer to the question asked, and yet score no marks.

If you plan an answer during your revision, do read the question set in the examination carefully, to make sure that you do know exactly what is required. Plan your answer to the question set: then include only relevant material in *your answer to this question*.

(g) Keep to the point

Some students, because they do not know the answer to the question set or do not read the question carefully, write more than is required and yet still do not answer the question. Perhaps remembering a relevant lecture, or having memorized several pages of notes on the subject, they insist on pouring forth all that they know. Instead they should be giving a considered answer: selecting and arranging only relevant points from their notes – and adding relevant information and ideas from other sources.

If asked to give a reasoned account of the circumstances leading to an event, a student might mention some things that happened before the event, describe the event in detail, and then discuss some after-effects. Yet there could be no marks for the description of the event, nor for discussing its after-effects, because the question did not ask for these things. And because only some circumstances leading to the event are mentioned, this part of the composition could not be considered well reasoned or complete. In other words, much time might be spent on this work and the student might feel pleased at having remembered so much and at covering so many pages with writing — yet very few marks could be awarded.

(h) Answer all parts of the question

When examinations are set the examiners prepare outlines of the answers they expect. Then they allocate marks to the parts of each answer or for each of the topics expected in a complete answer. You are likely to score most marks if, before starting to write, you prepare a plan that includes all the topics in the examiner's marking scheme (preferably in the same order). This is why you must read the question carefully and then think about what should be included in a complete and balanced answer. If some parts of the question are not answered you cannot score the marks available for these parts.

In structured questions, which indicate clearly the separate parts required in an answer, consider what is required in each part. Also, use your judgement in deciding how many marks are likely to be available for each part. Then allocate your time accordingly. If you spend too much time on one aspect of your answer you cannot score more than the number of marks allocated for this part. If you then spend too little time on other aspects you may not make the best use of your knowledge and so you are likely to score fewer marks than you should. For any aspects that you ignore, you can score no marks. You must appreciate the need to plan each answer, so that you can visualize the probable marking scheme. What does the examiner want to know *exactly*?

(i) Plan your answers

Some candidates are just not prepared to spend time on thinking and planning their answers. There is a temptation to write throughout the examination, and to write as much as possible, but this is usually a mistake. Planning is especially important in an examination because time is limited: as a result of spending some time on preparing a topic outline, all the remaining time can be used effectively (see Table 13.3).

Table 13.3 Allocating your time to a written answer

Activity	Time needed
Thinking about the question	3 min
Planning your answer	2 min
Writing (all the main points and enough explanation)	22 min
Checking	3 min

. Without thought and planning, information and ideas will probably not be presented in the most effective order, information on one topic may be included in different parts of the answer, information may be repeated, too much detail may be included on some topics and not enough on others, essential topics may be omitted, and the answer as a whole is unlikely to be well balanced. Such disorganized answers give an unfavourable impression and are difficult to mark.

Remember that marks are awarded according to a marking scheme, for relevance, completeness, and understanding. You must therefore decide on a limited number of main points (topics for your paragraphs) that the examiner will expect you to deal with in the limited time available for your answer. Any irrelevant material is likely to be deleted by the examiner. The inclusion of irrelevant material is not only a waste of time but it also serves as a smoke-screen – making relevant parts of an answer harder to find.

Prepare a plan or topic outline for each answer. You may do this immediately before starting the answer. Alternatively, you may prefer to plan all your answers at the beginning of the examination so that you can reconsider each outline later – immediately before writing your answer.

Planning will help you to remember things; and your topic outline will help you to get started and give direction to your work (see p. 107). Furthermore, additional points will come to mind as you write – according to plan.

You may decide to answer any compulsory questions first. Or you may answer first the questions you feel you can answer best. There are advantages in this, especially if you plan all your answers at the beginning of the examination, because it gives time for second thoughts about your other questions and you will probably benefit from reconsidering each question before you start to answer it. However, you should take care not to spend more time on what you think are the easy questions (at the start of an examination) so that you have *less time* for other questions which may need *more thought*.

(j) Display your knowledge

Some candidates omit things because they consider them too elementary. However, in examinations you score marks by displaying knowledge and understanding. Basic facts and ideas should be included, even if briefly and in passing, at appropriate places.

Similarly, in numerical questions the stages in your calculation must be shown. The examiner can then give marks for the part of your working that is correct – even if the answer is wrong. If you simply give the wrong answer you can score no marks.

(k) Make clear your understanding

Some candidates include relevant material in their answers but do not score high marks because they fail to make clear their understanding. In advanced examinations, particularly, it is not usually enough to simply demonstrate that you have a good memory. You should show your intelligence by planning each answer so that you can select relevant information and ideas and present them in an effective order.

Show that you understand what is required in each part of your answer by using words from the question at appropriate points in your answer: perhaps you can use them in topic sentences or as subheadings. Show your understanding in each paragraph by starting with the main point you wish to make in this paragraph (in a direct and forceful topic sentence), by including *enough* evidence or *explanation* and, if appropriate, by giving an example.

Use each part of your answer, and each paragraph, as an *opportunity to score marks* by adding only relevant information and ideas, and by making clear your understanding.

(l) Arrange your answer for easy marking

Some candidates give a jumbled answer, so that it is difficult for the examiner to tell whether or not each part of the question has been answered. Remember that the examiner may have many scripts to mark. Try to make the task as easy as possible so that it is easy for the examiner to give the marks you have earned.

The different kinds of questions, which may be set in course work and examinations, must be tackled in different ways. If a question is set in parts you are advised to arrange the parts of your answer in the same order as they appear in the question (see p. 157). Use letters (a), (b), (c), etc. if these are used in the question. Otherwise, select appropriate subheadings to act as signposts. This will help the examiner, who must work to a marking scheme (see p. 157), to find and mark each part of your answer. It will also help you to ensure that you answer all parts of the question and allocate your time appropriately to each part.

In other types of questions, clear paragraph breaks should indicate that you have said all that you intend to say about one topic and are just about to start a new topic. By planning you can deal adequately with each topic in one place – and this makes marking easier.

Start each answer at the top of a new page, unless you are instructed to do otherwise, but do not leave gaps within an answer. For example, do not leave a gap at the bottom of a page and then continue your answer on the next page. If you do, the examiner may read the first part of your answer and give a mark, thinking that you have finished. Then, finding the additional material, the examiner has to read this to see if the mark should be altered.

(m) Express your thoughts as clearly as you can

Some students use more words than are needed to convey their intended meaning precisely, probably because they do not know much about the subject and are trying to make their limited knowledge go a long way. Perhaps they think that marks are given for the number of pages filled with writing.

On the contrary, words which convey no meaning are like hurdles in a race: they hinder the reader's progress and so make it harder for the writer to convey meaning. Instead of displaying what is known, the extra words obscure meaning and give the immediate impression that little or nothing is known.

Examiners see too much of such padded writing – full of superfluous words, gobbledegook, surplusage, verbosity – and are unlikely to be impressed by the outward show of an excess of words. They may be annoyed if they have to search for the meaning, or, being unwilling to do so, may skim through the answer and then give a low mark.

(n) Write for easy reading

Remember that marks are given for the content and quality of your answers – not for their length. Write complete and carefully constructed sentences so that your meaning is clear. Some candidates make mistakes in their choice of words, in spelling, punctuation and grammar, or write a careless scrawl. All these things contribute to ambiguity and create an immediately unfavourable impression.

Examiners can give marks only for what they can read. And they can give marks only for what is written – not for what they think the candidate probably meant.

(o) Check your answers

Some candidates complete their last answer just as the instruction is given to stop writing. They leave no time for checking their work.

If at all possible, leave yourself time to read through all your answers. Check that you have answered all parts of each question. Check that every word is legible. Correct any slips of the pen, obvious spelling mistakes, or sentences that do not make sense. Check calculations, including substitutions in formulae, algebraic and arithmetic operations, and the position of each decimal point. Check that the result of your calculation is a reasonable answer to the question asked.

By making corrections yourself you can avoid being penalized for the mistakes. You may also be able to score extra marks by adding important points that you did not remember previously, and without which your answer would be incomplete.

(p) Use your time effectively

Concentrate fully: do not allow your mind to wander.

If a diagram is needed do not include unnecessary lines or waste time on shading. Distinguish the parts of a diagram by using coloured pencils and by clear labelling.

Remember, if you make a mistake or have second thoughts, that the quickest way to delete a number, letter, word or paragraph is to draw one line through it. Delete with an oblique line through single letters and with a horizontal line through words, so that you have space for corrections between your lines of writing. Do not waste your time on rubbing out or using white correcting fluid if it is quicker to delete and write again.

LEARN FROM YOUR OWN MISTAKES

Sometimes, after an examination, you realize that you have not done your best work. Nothing is to be gained by worrying about this immediately. Put the examination out of your mind. Try to relax. If necessary, prepare for the next examination.

If your script is returned, after marking, consider the examiner's comments to see if you can learn from them. You may be able to improve your study, revision and examination techniques. Consider where you went wrong so that you can try to avoid making the same kind of mistake again. Note where you lost marks because you failed to express your meaning unambiguously. Learn by trying to correct your mistakes. Seek help if necessary.

If possible, look at better answers prepared by other students. And in later revision sessions, attempt the questions you did not answer in the examination.

PREPARING FOR AN EXAMINATION

The day before an examination

1. Check again the date, time and location of your examination.
2. Prepare any writing materials or other equipment that you will need in the examination (e.g. pens with black or blue-black ink, sharp pencils, a ruler and an eraser, your watch, a calculator, and any books that you will be allowed to use).
3. If you decide to revise on the day before the examination do not work late.
4. Have a complete break, perhaps go for a walk, so that you can

relax before going to bed.

5. Set your alarm clock *and make other arrangements* to ensure that you get out of bed in good time (Fig. 13.1).

6. Try to have eight hours sleep. Relaxing on the day before, and a full night's sleep, will help you to be refreshed and alert throughout the examination. This will do more good, in helping you to think clearly and score marks, than would too much last minute revision.

Fig. 13.1 After a good night's sleep you will be refreshed and alert throughout the examination.

The day of an examination

1. Get up at the time you planned, so that you do not need to rush over washing and dressing, and you have time for a leisurely breakfast.

2. Check, before leaving, that you do have all the materials and equipment needed for the examination.

3. Arrive near to the examination room in good time but try to relax.

4. Go to the lavatory so that you will not need to leave the room during the examination.

5. Do not talk about the examination with other candidates.

6. Enter the examination room about ten minutes before the examination is due to start.

7. Find your place and arrange your writing materials and any other equipment on the working surface.

8. Write your name and other details, as instructed, in the spaces provided on the cover of your answer book.

9. If necessary, breathe in deeply – try to fill your lungs – then breathe out slowly. Do this a few times to help you to relax a little, but you should feel keyed up and ready to start.

TAKING EXAMINATIONS

Taking a theory examination

1. Read and *obey all the instructions* written on the front cover of your answer book. For example, you will probably be told to use a separate answer book for each part of the paper, to start each question at the top of a new sheet, and not to leave spaces within an answer or blank pages between the end of one answer and the start of the next.

2. *Check that you have been given the correct question paper*, that it is properly printed, and that you do have the whole paper.

3. *Read the instructions at the head of the paper*. Make sure you understand how much time is allowed, how many questions you should answer, and if there are any compulsory questions or any other restrictions on your choice.

4. *Read the whole paper* – all the questions – if you have a choice of questions. Look at both sides of each sheet to make sure that you do see all the questions.

5. *Select the questions that you can answer most fully*, then look again at the instructions at the head of the paper to check that your selection includes any compulsory questions and will be acceptable to the examiners.

6. *Allocate your time* to planning, writing and checking, so that you can do your best (i) to answer any compulsory questions; (ii) to answer the right number of questions, and (iii) to answer each question as fully as you are able in the time available for that question (see p. 155).

7. *Read each question again before you plan your answer.* Consider every word and phrase to make sure that you know exactly what the examiner wants to know, and for indications of the way the answer is to be presented (see p. 122). Plan your answer (see p. 123).

8. Before answering a question, write the number of the question conspicuously in the left hand margin at the top of a new page of your answer book, but *do not waste time copying out the question.*

9. You cannot spend much time on thinking about how to begin but a suitable starting point will probably become clear as you prepare the plan of your answer. In the first paragraph you will probably use some words from the question in a context which makes clear to the examiner that you do understand the question. Indeed, your first sentence or paragraph may give the essence of your answer.

10. Get to the point quickly and *keep to the point.* Work to your topic outline so that you can give an answer that is well balanced and well organized and so that you can make all your main points effectively in the time available – without digression or repetition (see p. 107).

11. *Respond to the words used in the question* (see p. 121). Do not make vague statements. Give reasons and examples. Include enough explanation.

12. Do not leave things out because you consider them too simple or too obvious (see p. 159). *The examiner cannot assume that you know anything* and can give marks only for what you write.

13. If you include anything that is not obviously relevant, explain why it is relevant.

14. Use small letters – (a), (b) etc. – or subheadings, or distinct paragraph breaks, as appropriate, to *make clear to the examiner where one aspect of the question has been dealt with and the next part of your answer begins.*

15. If a question is set in several parts, you must *spend enough time on each part of your answer.* You should also do your best to answer the parts in the order in which they are set, because the examiner will prefer to mark them in this order.

16. If the number of marks allocated to each part of a question is shown, next to the question, this should indicate not only how much time you should devote to each part of your answer but

also how many relevant points may be needed for an adequate answer to each part.

17. Make sure that any diagram is simple so that you can complete it quickly and neatly. Use coloured pencils, if necessary, to represent different things, but do not waste time on shading.

   Each diagram should be in the most appropriate place but should be numbered so that you can refer to it in other parts of your answer. If diagrams are necessary they should complement your writing, making explanation easier and enabling you to present information and ideas that could not be adequately presented in words alone. Effective diagrams should therefore reduce the number of words needed in your answer. *Do not waste time by conveying the information in both words and a diagram.*

18. *Make sure that your writing is legible* and use black or blue-black ink. Remember that coloured ink may be mistaken for the examiner's corrections.

   When you have completed your answer, and checked that you have included all points from your topic outline, it is a good idea to put a sloping line through your rough work so that the examiner can see at once that this is not part of your answer.

19. *Keep an eye on the time*, so that you can spend the right amount of time on each question (see p. 154) and have time to check all your answers towards the end of the examination (see p. 161).

20. Try to finish each question before starting the next, but if you get as far as you can with a question, or are unable to solve a problem, be prepared to leave it. Then remember to come back to it if you have time after answering other questions. You may well make more progress at your second attempt.

21. *Do not leave before the end.* If you have checked your work and have time to spare, look at each question again and at your topic outline (Fig. 13.2). Consider if there is anything you could add to improve any of your answers, so that you could score extra marks. Check that your name, and the other information required on the front page of your answer book, has been given.

22. When you leave the examination room nothing is to be gained from discussing the paper with other candidates. Try to think about other things, and to relax, until it is time to prepare for your next examination.

DO NOT LEAVE BEFORE THE END

Fig. 13.2   Make good use of all the time available in an examination.

Taking a practical examination

Prepare for your practical examinations by looking through your reports on practical exercises completed during the course, and by revising relevant theory. Also remember in theory examinations, where appropriate, to refer to your practical experience.

In practical examinations the basic rules are similar to those stated for theory examinations.

1. Obey all instructions written on the front cover of your answer book, and at the head of the question paper.
2. Read all the questions.
3. Decide which questions you will answer – if you have a choice.
4. Decide the order in which you will tackle the questions, then
5. Allocate your time, but remember . . .
6. In some practical examinations you may have time (e.g. while something is developing) to leave one question for a while and get on with another.
7. Also remember that you do not have to answer questions in the order in which they are set.

8. Read the question again before you start your answer, and follow any instructions carefully.

9. Spend as much time as is necessary on the easy questions – even if only a few marks are available for each of them. These few marks may help you to make a fail into a pass, or to make a good grade into a better one.

10. Make sure that your writing is legible and use black or blue-black ink.

11. Keep an eye on the time, and leave time to check all your answers towards the end of the examination.

12. Do not leave before the end.

Taking an oral examination

An oral or *viva voce* examination may follow the written examinations in any subject, and may allow an examiner to explore your strengths and weaknesses, revealed by your answers in written examinations, and to discuss your special study.

Dress appropriately, to meet the examiner, and try to relax before the interview. Walk confidently into the room but do not sit until you are invited to do so. Then sit upright, so that you feel comfortable but alert. The examiner will introduce himself and will ask your name – to make sure that you are the person expected at this time. As in normal conversation, be polite and self-confident but not aggressive. You must take the examination seriously but do smile occasionally: show your interest and enthusiasm. Be prepared to talk about your subject.

Speak clearly. Try not to answer simply yes or no. Give a little more information or explanation to show your knowledge and understanding, but do not go on for too long. If necessary give yourself time to think: you do not need to answer every question immediately. A few moments of thought and reflection may help you to collect your thoughts and summarize your reply. Leave the examiner free to ask further questions on this topic, or to move on to something else.

Failing examinations

Heading for failure?

1. Do you attend all organized classes?
2. Do you review your notes soon after each class?
3. Are you doing appropriate background reading, using appropriate reading skills, and trying to fill gaps in your knowledge?
4. Do you ask for help when necessary?
5. Do you prepare for classes?
6. Do you revise regularly?
7. Do you complete all exercises set for homework, and hand them in for assessment on time?
8. Do you have difficulty in organizing compositions or in expressing yourself clearly in writing?
9. Do you consider the comments and advice written on your assessed work?
10. Are you devoting enough time to all aspects of your subjects that will be assessed in course work and examinations?
11. Are you devoting enough time to recreation, and looking after yourself in other ways?
12. Are you working hard enough?

Assess your own progress. Are you likely to achieve a grade that is a true indication of your ability? If this self-evaluation causes you to decide that your performance is unsatisfactory, consider what you should do to bring about an improvement.

Failing

If you fail an examination, do not try to find excuses or to blame others. Perhaps you simply did not work hard enough, or did not make effective use of your study and leisure time, or did not revise regularly, or did not make effective use of your time in examinations. Recognizing where you went wrong is the first step towards putting things right – if you decide to take the examinations again or to take some other course.

Perhaps you will decide to do something else and make new plans. However, do not make a hasty decision. First take a break and then reconsider your position.

Appendix A

Choosing a course

You probably studied a variety of subjects at school, as part of a broad education, and then selected certain subjects to take in examinations. Studying these subjects may have helped you to decide what to do next. More than this, it provided a foundation for your further studies. You would have encountered difficulties if you had decided, later, to work for a more advanced examination or to make a career in a field that is normally based on the study of other subjects.

These things are true at each stage in your formal education. If you wish to specialize in a particular subject in your later years at college, you may have to study this subject and others (called pre-requisites) in the earlier years. On the other hand, if you are not sure which is to be your main subject you should try to take a choice of subjects in the first year that will enable you to decide, later, to specialize in one or two of them.

Before starting any course of study, if you have a particular career in mind, talk to people who already have the qualification at which you are aiming. Also, look at the booklets on careers published, for example, by different professional bodies and institutes.

Consider what kind of course you should take and then find out what courses of this kind are available. You can do this by writing to the colleges at which you think you might like to study. Such enquiries should be made as far in advance of your preferred starting date as possible, so that you can complete your applications and submit them before any closing dates.

The entry requirements for advanced courses are such that, having satisfied them, you should be able to cope with the more advanced work. However, try to assess your own suitability for this course. If you are still at school, your teachers will help you to understand what may be involved in further studies of their subjects. Nothing is to be gained by attempting things which, for you, will be impossible.

CORRESPONDENCE COURSES

To be able to study in your own home may be an advantage, depending upon your circumstances, but there are disadvantages.

Disadvantages of postal tuition

Study notes prepared by other people should not be as useful to you as your own lecture notes (see p. 41). Also, there is more to be gained from lectures and other organized classes than a neat set of notes (see p. 13). The home-based student may also suffer, both academically and socially, from lack of contact with other students.

At college the lecturers and other students help to set the pace. In postal tuition you receive regular advice and instructions, and you will have to submit completed work for marking, but – even more than in other kinds of courses – the driving force must be yourself.

Self discipline is necessary. It is best to read quickly through the material, as soon as it arrives, and to consider what needs to be done. Then decide when you will do it. Make your own notes and leave space for additions when you undertake additional reading. Make notes of any difficulties or questions (see p. 47). Start work on any exercises and plan to complete them in time (see Table 4.5, p. 33).

The main problem for a student taking a correspondence course is isolation. There is no one you can easily turn to for advice, except in so far as the librarians in your local library are able to help. However, some correspondence courses are so organized that students can meet their tutors, and other students living locally, and there may also be short residential courses.

Advantages of postal tuition

1. Correspondence courses are available to people who live in remote areas or who are unable to attend college because of

family ties or incapacity, or who live in places where no suitable part-time course is available.

2. Time can be devoted to study instead of to travel.

3. You can choose your own time for study, in relation to other commitments such as full-time employment.

4. You can work at your own pace.

5. You are provided with notes that will help you to prepare for a particular examination; and if you are not very good at note-making these may be better than your own notes would be.

6. There may be relevant broadcast films and talks, and some of these may be designed to support the course you are taking.

7. Regular set work is planned for you. If you keep up with your work, week by week, your progress is monitored and you receive comments and advice.

8. Correspondence courses give a second chance or an opportunity for further education for people who are already employed, but before undertaking such a course consider what will be involved and what other demands there will be on your time. Determination will be needed and there is no point in starting any course unless you are prepared to find the time that will be required.

PART-TIME COURSES

The main advantage of a part-time course is that you can start upon a career and continue your education at the same time. Part-time courses also enable students, who for one reason or another cannot attend a full-time course, to continue their education, meet lecturers and other students who have similar interests to their own, ask for advice, use facilities, and obtain qualifications that will help them to make progress in their careers. They also enable qualified people to obtain further or higher qualifications in the early years of their subsequent employment or to take refresher courses after they have been employed for some years. However, a part-time course is more demanding than a full-time course; it is likely to leave you less time to devote to personal relationships and recreation – and is not to be entered into lightly.

Part-time and correspondence courses are particularly attractive to people who already have many commitments (e.g. full-time or part-time employment, a house to maintain, children to care for). Such people, before committing themselves to study, should decide whether or not they will find the time that will be needed to attend all classes (see p. 26) and for private study (see p. 34). Are they prepared to give up other things? Will they receive cooperation and encouragement from their family or friends, which will be necessary if they are to have (i) regular free evenings or weekends to attend organized classes, (ii) time to visit libraries, and (iii) periods of quiet study?

FULL-TIME COURSES

If you decide upon a full-time course, consider what type of course to take. Most full-time courses include periods of attendance at college (in term time) and periods away from college (in vacations); but in cooperative education or sandwich courses, periods of full-time attendance at college alternate with periods of training in relevant paid employment. Such courses take longer (perhaps four years instead of three). Apart from the longer time needed, you may have difficulty in settling down at college after a long break in your studies. However, the period of appropriate employment should not be regarded as a break in your studies; it provides opportunities to relate college work to a particular career, and to devote some time in the evenings and at weekends to the revision and consolidation of college work and to background reading. If these opportunities are taken, the habit of studying is not lost during the training period; and you return to college with a good basis for the next year of the course.

If asked what you hoped to gain from a period of further or higher education, you would probably reply that you wanted to obtain a particular qualification. You might add that you intended to do as well as possible in your final examinations. To obtain employment you would also need a good reference or recommendation from your Head of Department or from another senior member of the academic staff of your college. If you take a course that includes periods of relevant paid employment you will gain experience, learn to get along with people, become more self-reliant away from home or college, and so gain in maturity of outlook. You will also hope to obtain a good reference or recommendation from a senior member of staff at the training establishment, when the time comes to look for permanent employment.

Appendix B

Books for your bookshelf

1. Look at the books included in your reading lists, and at other recommended publications, as suggested on p. 80. Be prepared to buy up-to-date textbooks for each aspect of your course. Make sure that each one is appropriate for your course and for the stage you have reached in your studies. If there is a choice, select books which you find easy to read and understand. Your lecturers will be pleased to offer advice. And you may find it helpful to talk to students who passed the course last year.

   You will need a good textbook from the start of each course of lectures. It will complement the lectures and should be on your bookshelf – available for preliminary reading before lectures and for immediate reference.

2. Buy a dictionary that gives the spelling, pronunciation and meaning of each word, its uses in current English, its derivatives (words derived from it), and its derivation: for example, *Chambers' Twentieth Century Dictionary* (Chambers, Edinburgh), *Collins' Dictionary of the English Language* (Collins, Glasgow), *The Concise Oxford Dictionary of Current English* (Oxford University Press, London), or *Websters' New Collegiate Dictionary* (Merriam, Massachusetts).

3. Many students are clever enough to understand their work and yet unable to organize and communicate their thoughts effectively. They need help with their writing more than further instruction in their chosen subjects. If you have found this book helpful, and accept that you need further help with your writing,

study these handbooks: Barrass, R. (1982) *Students Must Write: a guide to better writing in course work and examinations*, Methuen & Co Ltd, London and New York. Gowers, E. (1973) *The Complete Plain Words*, 2nd edn revised by Sir Bruce Fraser, HMSO, London.

4. For an audio-visual introduction to study techniques, see: Main, A.N. (1977) *Study Patterns – a videotape series*, Centre for Educational Practice, University of Strathclyde, Glasgow.

5. If you have a study problem and need help or further advice, see a member of the academic staff or a study counsellor at your college (see p. 9).

If you wish to discuss a personal problem see your personal tutor or academic adviser, or any other member of the academic staff whom you find approachable and sympathetic (see p. 19). You will find that most teachers accept that counselling is part of their work and are pleased to help.

If you need advice on a medical problem, or treatment for any disease or illness, see your doctor without delay.

Lecturers and tutors, who meet students regularly and are frequently asked for advice on study and personal problems, will find many helpful suggestions in: Main, A.N. (1980) *Encouraging Effective Learning: an approach to study counselling*, Scottish Academic Press, Edinburgh.

Index